Conflict Resolution History of Zimbabwe.

Obediah Dodo (PhD)

Governance & Leadership (Unilus)

Title

Conflict Resolution History of Zimbabwe.

Sub-title

Conflict Resolution

Year of Publication

2018

Copyright

Copyright © Obediah Dodo (2017)

All rights reserved. No part of this publication may be reproduced, stored in a retrieval system or transmitted in any form or by any means, electronic, mechanical, photocopying, recording or otherwise, be lent, sold, hired-out or otherwise circulated without express written consent of the author.

Dedication

For all the people who continually inspire me to understand conflict resolution.

And to Nokutenda and Paidamoyo, my beautiful daughters.

Acknowledgements

All the chapters went through peer-reviews. I wish to thank all the reviewers for their objective comments and corrections. I would lie to acknowledge all the assistance that I got from the staff at the National Archives in Harare; continually helping me to find the most relevant material.

The field of conflict resolution has separated me from my family as it keeps me glued to my researches. It has again starved my family of my love and attention. However, they have all steadfastly remained honest advisors, friends and dependents. I thank them for all the support.

I also want to thank my workmates who have always supported and encouraged me to keep writing.

Contents Page

Foreword

The book is about the development of conflict resolution as a practice in Zimbabwe since time immemorial. It is written against a realisation that there has not been any consolidated literature that specifically focuses on the history of conflicts and their respective ways of attending to them. Various scholars have written about conflicts in Zimbabwe since the early states prior to colonialism. However, they lack a dimension that focuses on how these conflicts were resolved systematically and how those approaches were nurtured and preserved over time.

This book focuses on how various approaches of resolving conflicts were developed and preserved. It also looks at how traditional Shona conflict resolution means were later fused with some of the exogenous approaches culminating into more polished and time-relevant endogenous approaches. The book however acknowledges that most of the indigenous conflict resolution approaches were valuable. It also recognises that they were supported by cultural and social values, customs and philosophies that were acceptable in the respective societies with reverence, transparency, participation, societal unity, coordination, peaceful co-existence, patience and self-effacement amongst others.

It is realised that while conflict resolution as a practice has always been part and parcel of the Shona people since the early states prior to colonisation, very little has been said about women in as far as conflict resolution is concerned. Therefore, this book traces the history of the Shona people way beyond the time that the Europeans named them as such in 1839 going in some instances as far back as the Moroccan Heights settlements before the attempted Berberisation of Africa. The study seeks to find the real place of women in the politics of the indigenous Shona people.

It is acknowledged that while the indigenous Shona people had their ways of attending to conflicts, over time; several other factors intervened thus transforming the original practices of the people. The coming of the Ndebele and the Europeans into the lives of the Shona people meant that a new approach to conflict resolution was to be created. These approaches gradually fused with the endogenous approaches. In the book, it is noted that exogenous approaches to conflict resolution were facilitated through the introduction of western education which outrightly transformed the ideologies, perceptions, principles and values of the indigenous people. The effects of the coming of the foreigners and their forms of education and religions are also discussed in the book.

The last chapter in the book discusses the challenges to the concept of conflict resolution in general and how it was applied in the indigenous traditional Shona culture in particular. The book notes that the challenges varied from structural, political, economic, and social to religious. It also looks at some specific barriers to the effective and efficient application of the methods. The entire book however tries to link all the concepts from chapter one to the last for coherence. It also relates all the arguments bringing them to a common position where any reader can comprehend the scope and argument of the discussion.

About the Author

Obediah Dodo holds a doctorate in Governance and Leadership from the University of Lusaka, Zambia. He also holds a masters' degree in Peace and Governance, a Post-Graduate diploma in Peace and Governance, Post-Graduate Diploma in Tertiary Education, B. A. in English and Communication and a Diploma in Journalism. He lectures at Bindura University in the Department of Peace and Governance. Obediah has published over fifty-five journal papers and fifteen full books. Dr Obediah Dodo has research interests in conflict resolution, youth and family violence and election management. He sits on various journal and civil society boards.

Acronyms

ANC	African National Congress
BSAC	British South Africa Company
JZM	Jesuit Zambezi Mission
LMS	London Missionary Society
NLHA	Native Land Husbandry Act
SDA	Seventh Day Adventist
TCA	Tribal Courts Act
ZANLA	Zimbabwe African National Liberation Army
ZANU	Zimbabwe African National Union
ZAPU	Zimbabwe African People's Union
ZIPRA	Zimbabwe People's Revolutionary Army

Definition of Terms

Backward – This refers to a society that believes and lives in archaic and long abandoned practices and world. People in this situation reject change for the better clinging on to the old systems.

Civilisation – This is a state of being appropriately placed in the right era in terms of development. With civilisation, people must be able to relate with the prevailing lifestyles, practices and viewpoints and not be conversant with the long discarded systems.

Conflict Resolution – this is a deliberate initiative meant to either quell a potentially volatile situation or institute conditions that address a prevailing conflict regardless of the mechanism's sustainability.

Development – This is when both people and their infrastructure are changing to suit the prevailing times. This is an ability to adapt to dynamism in society. It is a movement from a lower level of civilisation to a higher one that also considers democracy, human rights, and good governance.

Endogenous – These are community embedded, culturally acceptable and long-time practices by a particular community.

Indigenous – This refers to either local people or practices. It carries with it such elements as knowledge, relationship, and continuity.

Natives – These are indigenous people of an area. The term was loosely used by the colonialists during the 1890s derogatively to refer to the communities that were found in Zimbabwe by the Europeans.

Shona people – these are the original people who lived on the plateau and were named Tshona by the Ndebele in 1838-40 defining all ethnic groups that shared particular traits especially the Rozvi.

Traditional – In this book, traditional refers to early and community imbedded practices by the indigenous people of Zimbabwe. The term carries nothing derogatory in it.

Zimbabwe – This refers to early stone structures that were built by the indigenous early Zimbabweans as barriers to external aggression. It also refers to the present-day state after it was named in 1980.

CHAPTER ONE

CONFLICT RESOLUTION: AN INTRODUCTION

Introduction

Conflict resolution is a concept that has been a part of most communities and governance systems the world over. Zimbabwe has not been an exception. Since time immemorial, Zimbabwe has had its various methods of resolving conflicts, which suited the local cultures, religious beliefs and ethnic groups. This chapter, as an introduction to the book, seeks to explain the various aspects around conflict resolution and how they sustainably worked in the respective communities. The chapter also traces the history of conflict resolution in Zimbabwe since the early states looking at some of the events and activities that contributed to the transformation of the applied methods.

Background

As a lecturer of peace studies, my daily experience is that most new peace students think that conflict resolution is a very new and imported concept so much so that they are excited to attend introductory lectures. It is only when I take them for a course on endogenous conflict resolution systems that they realize that the concepts are as old as humanity. However, they enjoy the course. The questions that most people have often asked are; 'What is conflict resolution and how did it come into being? Why is it that the concept is often talked about by the Europeans and yet Africans are the most affected by conflicts? Have our forefathers never had their own conflict resolution systems that were specific and appropriate for the local challenges?' It is these questions and several others that that for some time, I thought about coming up with a lengthy and elaborate discussion on the origins and the development of conflict resolution in Africa in general and Zimbabwe in particular. I seek to introduce this discussion from an African perspective and not European as is the usual norm. I hope that the discussion opens more opportunities for more researches on the same subject matter given that this discussion presents the other side of the account. This is against a background of a distorted history by early emotionally charged liberation war leaders who probably wanted to depict their cause as heroic and dire. Remember that the Zimbabwean history was re-written between 1969 and 1972 by the ZANU Department of Education primarily to present a story that could attract sympathy and support from both national and international citizens. The First teachers then were Sheba Tavarwisa and Pedzisai who opened the first school in 1973 at Chifombo in Zambia. To ensure that the school curriculum propagated what the nationalists wanted, the Liberation movement's Department of Education headed by Ernest Kadungure was enlarged bringing in the Research Department which was headed by Ephraim Chitofu (Comrade Mushatagotsi) and deputized by Fay Chung[1]. The defining falsehoods and exaggerations therefore wash away the credence in the history.

Conflicts are common and ubiquitous in all societies. They manifest in different forms; minute and large-scale, they arise within individuals, in small families, villages, work-places, community programmes, inter-states and between leaders amongst others. At the end of the day, what is required is an amicable long-term solution which is favourable to all the

[1] Mahamba I. (2016) 'Education Curriculum has to be in our Hands' p.12, Sunday Mail, Zimpapers, Harare.

parties and which influences development and establishment of more relationships.

Zimbabwe attained its political independence in 1980 from the British colonialists who had run it from the 1890s and had named it Rhodesia in 1898 after securing the Order in Council from the British government. Before the independence of 1980, the country was called Rhodesia following the dissolution of a federation that had existed for over 40 years during which it was called Southern Rhodesia. However, before colonialism, the same country was not yet demarcated using the Berlin Conference boundaries which subsequently created Rhodesia. Therefore, it had no 'an all-encompassing' name. It must however be pointed out that there was a proposition by Theodore Bent in his paper on Zimbabwe and its ruins that was presented at the Royal Geographical in the 1880s, that the name Zimbabwe originated from the following; 'Z' stood for a Bantu root for a village; '*Umzi*' is a Zulu word for a collection of villages; '*Zimbab*' meant a great kraal; '*We*' was an exclamation. It therefore implied that Zimbabwe meant '*Here is the great kraal*'. However this discussion wishes to side with a commentary in the Rhodesian Herald of Saturday 14 January 1893[2], which critiqued and discarded Bent's proposition for its lack of reason, meaning and background and that Bent's period of study in Zimbabwe was not long enough to allow him to make such conclusions given his weak language proficiency. Similarly, the discussion argues that Mongameli Mabona's theory regarding Zimbabwe is also weak. Mabona was a Catholic priest who argues that the name Zimbabwe was a distorted Nguni word for *Zimbiwambiwe* which is a short form for '*Kwazintaba Zimbiwambiwe*'

---

[2] The Rhodesian Herald of Saturday 14 January 1893 titled 'Zimbabwe Origins' p.2.

meaning 'mountains full of mines'. This author also presents an argument to the effect that the country though not in the same geographical boundaries was known as *Chivavarira*[3] meaning 'land that had long been dreamt of'. There were some Europeans who did not believe that Zimbabwe ruins had been built by indigenous people given the artistic, creativity, perfection and architectural acumen exhibited. Actually, in 1872, a German geologist Karl Mauch argued that the infrastructure had been built by what he termed 'civilised people'[4] and not the indigenous inhabitants. All these arguments by different scholars simply point to the fact that the origins of the Zimbabwe ruins are still a mystery to some foreign scholars.

Conflict Resolution

This is a broad concept that has been defined differently by various scholars depending on one's background politically, ideologically, economically, and socially. However, from an endogenous conflict resolution stand-point, the concept must be understood as any means that seeks to ensure that any conflict is sustainably and peacefully attended. How the conflict is attended to may be in any form which is acceptable to the community concerned. These measures may range from violent approaches, peaceful, discussion approaches, to spilling of blood for as long as it ensures that the other part is removed from the conflict puzzle. Basically, conflict resolution is about sustainably ending a conflict through whatever means possible.

---

[3] Author's interview with villagers in Chidodo and Tsokoto villages in 1994.

[4] Mtshali V. B. (1967) Rhodesia: Background to Conflict, SA

The Origins of the Bantu

The Bantu people are one of the several groups that are found in Africa today; the continent inhabited by an all-dark people commonly referred to as black people by some racists. Originally, the continent was inhabited by basically three races; Bushmanoids, Negroids, and Pygmanoids before the Caucasoids arrived from Europe and Asia around ten thousand years BC. The coming of the Caucasoids into Libya also triggered the migration of the Negroids to Europe[5]. The original races cross-bred the Bantu people who were a quiet and peaceful people before they scattered all over the continent leaving the latter in the north[6]. The history of Africa as a continent and the origins of its name are not really known. However, snippets of information present various arguments with regards to the origins of the name as argued by Samkange[7] who says the name could have come from Afer, son of Hercules or Africos or Ifricos the son of Abraham. Samkange also talks of other beliefs; attribution of the name to another Afer, a descendant of Goliath the giant who is believed to have fled from Asia to Africa after the killing of his father by David, or that the name came from the land between Africa and Sicily. Other scholars also argue that the name came from the fact that the original people were settled on the entire land north of the Sahara desert (minus Egypt) which was called Libya[8]. These people were called

[5] Diop C. A. (1968) 'Negro Nations and Culture' in *Problems in African History*, ed. Collins R. O., Englewood Cliffs, NJ, Prentice-Hall.

[6] Nickerson J. G. (1961) A Short History of North Africa, Biblo and Tannen, NY.

[7] Samkange S. (1971) African Saga: A Brief Introduction to African History, Harare Pub. House, Salisbury.

Afri and the early Arabs to invade Libya then called it '*Afri-ca*' the '*land of the Afri*'.

To understand the history of the now Zimbabwe and its people, it is imperative that a brief reflection on the Bantu people be made. Various scholars who include Professor Stanlake Samkange, Professor Joseph Greenberg and Professor Malcolm Guthrie believe that the Bantu people must have originated from one source; the central Cameroons and the east central Nigeria. This is based on various factors including linguistic evidence. The other evidence shows that the Bantu dispersal produced a dynamic population explosion which subsequently led to a cultural revolution introducing the use of iron tools for agriculture and weapons for hunting and military purpose. It is reported that amongst other reasons, the Bantu's move down south was a response to the coming in of the Barbers from the north.

As the Bantu spread southwards passing through vast grass-lands which are now commonly referred to as *Guruuswa[i]*, they found the land inhabited by hunter-gatherers and pastoralists like Bushmen, Pygmies, Dorobo, Hottentots, Tatog and the Iraqw[9]. However in the study of Niger-Congo and the origins of the Bantu people, there is reference to what is thought to be the origins of the Narrow Bantu in northwest

[8] Welch G. (1949) North African Prelude, Morrow, NY.

[9] See Samkange.

Jackson J. J. (1970) *Introduction to African Civilisation*. Hyde Park; NY, University Books.

[10] Waters J. R. (1989) *Bantoid Overview: Niger-Congo,* Bendor Samuel (eds) University Press of America.

Grassfields[10]. According to this study, this land is to the south of Nigeria and Cameroon. Along the way, the Bantu acquired skills to grow crops and hunt. As they moved further down, they were forced to sharpen their diplomatic skills each time they were involved in some conflicts over free passage, water, pastures, land, and hunting rights amongst others. As these groups moved, those who were too old to continue moving and the weaker would settle while the stronger continued with the journey. This saw a few strongest reaching the south end of the continent before they later migrated northwards fleeing Tshaka Zulu's barbaric and autocratic leadership later in the 1820s. This to some extent explains why groups in the southern part of Africa are stronger than those in the upper areas and as you go further up to the north. Another argument from oral evidence point out that the early Bantu migrated from Mesopotamia under the leadership of Murenga and his two children Nyakasikana and Mindudzepasi later known as Chaminuka. It was Murenga's influence and leadership that led to the establishment of a country originally called Chivavarira that shared borders with Kambiya and Mazambuko.

'Dzimbabwe' to Zimbabwe

Historically, the country was multi-ethnic as it was comprised of the Manyika and the Ndau in the east, the Zezuru and the Korekore in the central and northern parts, the Tshangani and the Venda in the south and south east and the Tonga in the north, the Karanga in central southern parts while the Ndebele who came later settled in the south-west and in the process corrupted some Karanga and subsequently created the Kalanga who then settled in south-western areas of the country. The society according to Lewis[11] was pluralistic in nature divided along ethnic, religious, cultural, linguistic and regional differences. According to some of the early structural functionalist anthropologists, the now Zimbabwean society was an assortment of ethnic groups that were categorized and divided by distinct cultural indicators. According to various scholars who include Beach[12], the people who lived in these early states were uncivilized if it were to be defined from a civilized and modernized stand-point[ii].

According to researches; scientific and non-scientific, it has been established that there have been at least five cultures that have existed in Zimbabwe since the 900AD[13]. It is these cultures that define the settlement of the indigenous people in all the states to have ever existed. Between 850 and 830AD, there was the Gukurume culture which existed to the south of the central plateau while the Leopards Kopje existed from 940AD. Leopards Kopje was in the south west of the plateau. The other culture to have existed was the Gumanye from 1090AD. It was to the south of the plateau in the middle of Mutilikwe, Tokwe and Lundi rivers. There was also Harare culture between 1150 and 1180AD and this existed in the central plateau between Hunyani and Umfuli valleys. The last culture to have been identified was the Musengezi which was further to the north and west of the plateau and it existed from 1210AD.

For over a thousand years, the land area then was defined by various great states of the likes of Great Zimbabwe in Masvingo which started off as Gukurume before it was corrupted to Gokomere, the Mutapa state

---

[11] Lewis W. A. (1965) Politics in West Africa. Oxford University, Oxford.

[12] Beach D. N. (1980) The Shona and Zimbabwe, 900 to 1850: An Outline of Shona History, Gweru, Mambo Press

[13] See Beach D. N.

in Dande, the Rozvi state, the Torwa state and finally the Ndebele state in Bulawayo which defeated the last reigning state before the coming in of the European colonialists in the 1830s. Before the coming of both the Ndebele and Europeans into the now Zimbabwe, the land was not known as Zimbabwe or Rhodesia. The inhabitants were also not known as the Shona people as they are called today. Rather, the land was simply identified by the states that existed then while the people in the respective states were identified by their ethnic origins and cultural practices. In other words, the local groupings were not conscious of their differences and similarities culturally or otherwise. They also did not have particularly identifying group names. However, other sources suggest that the present day Zimbabwe boundaries were drawn following the Mutapa state area of jurisdiction[14]. When the Ndebele moved in from the south fleeing the *mfecane* war, they found some people whom they just referred to as *Intshonalanga*. However, because all these ethnic groups' languages shared some structural and phonetic similarities, the first European academics to arrive referred to these groups as the *Tshona* before they gradually corrupted it to Shona as they could not pronounce the Ndebele word. This marked the birth of the Shona people and it was around 1838-39. Like I indicated above, it was the early Europeans who named the local ethnic groups as posited by David Beach and Terrance Ranger[15]. Beach presents that the Korekore was a term given to mean the people of the North and Northwest while the Zezuru meant people who lived in a high plateau around Mazowi Valley[iii]. Beach goes on to argue

---

[14] Ranger T. (1999). Voices from the Rocks. Bloomington: Indiana University Press. Also see Beach

[15] Missionaries, Migrants and the Manyika: The Invention of Ethnicity in Zimbabwe in *The Creation of Tribalism in Southern Africa,* UCP, California.

that the name Ndau was a pejorative pseudonym given to the people of the Eastern border by the invading Gaza Nguni. However, I wish to point out that none of the researchers has been able to explain the sources of their claims hence remain hazy and unreliable. I therefore treat the information as work in progress.

The early states had built some unique form of approach to external intrusion and confrontation. It must be noted that these early states were involved in international trade with other states from as far as the Far East and China from as early as 1290 till the 1600. One such ancient formal trading system was the Mukumvura (now Mukumbura), led by Ribeiro and operated between Tete and Upper Mazowe since the 1860s. It was only abandoned when the trading concession was given to *Companhia da Zambezia*, a Portuguese company. It was because of this trade that some conflicts erupted. Therefore, over time, the local people were then forced to come up with some form of diplomacy which helped them to resolve conflicts especially with the foreign traders who appeared to be more civilized and literate than them. It had also proved that violent confrontation was not necessary for basically two reasons; the foreigners had superior weaponry and that the locals also benefitted from the trade economically, socially, politically and militarily. This is the era when an indigenous form of conciliation and arbitration were developed.

The coming of the Europeans in the early nineteenth century to some extent created a bond between the local peoples as they realized a need to face a common enemy who threatened the existence of their cultural systems. Earlier on I said these local people were not distinctively separated by any form of physical structures except cultural markers.

However, following the coming of the Europeans and their attempts at bringing down their systems, they eventually shared notes before they then confronted them militarily. It was after this had failed that different dialects, languages, cultural systems, and other rites were merged to create 'new systems' that fostered conflict resolution in communities. Such new systems came in the form of treaties that were somehow forced on the indigenous peoples. Treaties literally created some understanding between parties over an activity and did put in place some assurance that none of the signatories was to renege on the agreement. In 1875, the Hwata headquarters in Dandamira hills (presently Dorking farm, in Concession), north of the plateau was attacked by Mzilikazi in his expansionist drive[16]. As a result, Hwata Gwindi surrendered before he passed on in 1880. In 1889, his lieutenant roped in the services of the African soldiers led by Manuel Antonio de Sousa, *Guvheya* who then offered guns and a Portuguese flag in an alliance against the Ndebele. After the victory, the Hwata title was given to Mutimumwe on condition that the Portuguese also had a stake[17]. To a large extent, treaties and alliances resolved and even prevented conflicts in the communities.

It was however till December 1560 when a missionary called father Gonzalo da Silveira moved into one of the states that some more conflicts were recorded following his successes in converting some members of the Mutapa royal family to Christianity. Because of the emerging ideological and religious beliefs, the state began to witness

---

[16] According to original and unedited version of a diary by the Native Commissioner's office in Mazoe Fort, 1875.

[17] Beach D. N. (1995) An Innocent Woman, Unjustly Accused? Charwe Medium of the Nehanda Mhondoro Spirit and the 1896-7 Central Shona Rising in Zimbabwe. History Seminar Paper 98.

conflicts which eventually led to the breakaway of other areas. Besides these ideological and religious influenced conflicts, trade also brought in a fair share of violent wars. However over time, the Rozvi state in the central-southern parts of the country resorted to trading with the foreigners through marketing agents called '*Vashambadzi*'. It must be noted that the first Arabs came to Zimbabwe in 900AD while the Portuguese came in 1500AD.

Historical accounts suggest that the majority of the early northerners and now Shona peoples were generally peaceful compared to their Ndebele counterparts. However, like all other societies, they frequently engaged in conflicts and wars over various issues. The coming of the early Christian missionaries changed their approaches to conflict and conflict resolution given that the missionaries preached peace, harmony and tolerance. The missionaries' messages were meant to pacify the locals' determination to defend their areas and resources from exploitation. Be that as it may, the message of peace and tolerance played an important role in the defence systems of the local peoples as the indigenous had developed an interest in securing places in what the missionaries called 'heaven' after their death. So it was the fear of death and the fear of being sent to hell that the locals changed their behaviours.

In this discussion, the area that is being discussed will be referred to as Zimbabwe and the most prominent ethnic groups are the Zezuru, Karanga, Manyika, Ndebele and the Ndau (though not in any particular order). The main communication languages by these groups are Shona and Ndebele.

Early Ethnic Groups in the Early States

Zimbabwe as a state only assumed that name in 1980. Prior to that, it was called Rhodesia though for a brief period in 1978, it was named Zimbabwe-Rhodesia. The name Rhodesia came into being after the British had colonized the early states which were but not bound together by any formal political structures. The name Zimbabwe was suggested by a ZANU nationalist called Michael Mawema in 1961 during a secret political meeting and it was a derivation from the term *Dzimbabwe.*

The various political systems were made up of closely-knit ethnic groups or rather large family groups which shared the following amongst others; similar dialects, culture, religious beliefs, agricultural practices, marriage rites, totemic values and heritage. Some of the most prominent ethnic groups to have been recorded since early civilization excluding those that were brought in by the coming of the Ndebele people in the 1830s include; the Zezuru in the central plateau and now Harare and the surrounding highland areas, Korekore in the north and north-east of the plateau, Karanga in the south and south west of the plateau, Ndau further to the east of Manyika, Manyika to the east of the plateau, Maungwe in now Rusape, Budya in Mutoko, Doma in Mbire/Chewore, and the Tonga in Kariva. There were also the Tshangani to the south-east of the Karanga, Majindwi to the south east of Manyika, Mahera in now Buhera, and the Nambya in Mosi-a-Tunya, Barwe in the now Marondera/Macheke areas, and the Shangwe next to Karanga, Varozvi in Gukurume, Vambire in the now Wedza, Nhowe in the now Murewa and Bocha in the now Marange area.

The early inhabitants of the land now Zimbabwe were peculiar in some form. They had amongst others managed to construct a '*dzimbabwe*' (stone house) which the early Europeans described as a mystery, riddle and an enigma of the state. Besides, they had also demonstrated a unique intellectual capacity and organizational skill through a complex religious concept connected with the worship of the Supreme Divine Being. Another unique skill was also presented in the economic sphere where states had a sound economic base founded on agriculture and trade with Arabs from the east coast[18]. It is important that I highlight the importance of the Europeans' trade visits to the continent and Zimbabwe in particular: the visits led to colonization.

Colonization of Africa and the Conflict

The indigenous people's trade with the Europeans gave the latter an opportunity to realize the beauty and the vast resources that were in the continent. The debate over colonialism has always brought in a diversity of views and arguments with some blaming it for the underdevelopment of Africa while others credit it for the few positive developments in Africa. It also has to be mentioned that our endeavor to understand the history of conflict resolution in Zimbabwe can only be made easy if we also understand colonialism, which apparently came soon after slave trade was abolished.

The scramble for Africa began as soon as the missionaries had established their work stations and had learnt some indigenous languages for communication purposes. To these and their fellow back in Europe, having colonies in Africa was seen as a means of acquiring national prestige, keeping the scales of the distribution of power in Europe even and mollifying wounded national pride. A rush for a territory in Africa ensued subsequently leading to the Berlin 1884-85 conference which

[18] July R. (1970) A History of the African People. Scribner, NY.

drew arbitrary boundaries. These boundaries sometimes put people of a single tribe into different states or would lump together into one state people who should have been in separate states. What has to be realized however is that colonization was not necessarily undertaken by governments but by private companies specifically created for the task. Respective governments legally had no control over these private companies that would have only secured charters for operations of the colonies. Also important to note is that the Berlin conference discussed a noted increase in fraudulent treaties and bogus purchases of land from unsuspecting African leaders. The cupidity, conspiracy, cutthroat competition and rivalry that characterised the activities of many of the foreign agencies generated friction, hatred and animosity both among Europeans as well as African leaders. Therefore, the conference formulated rules that governed colonization; that claims to protectorates in Africa should be formally registered and notification given to members. Besides, the conference also agreed that there would be freedom of navigation along the Niger and Congo rivers. An interesting inter-European states conflict was recorded in Zimbabwe pitting the Anglo against the Lusophone interests on the Zimbabwe eastern side boundary. The conflict between British and Portuguese with regards to the delimitation of the area of Manicaland arose from the interpretation of Article 2 of the Anglo-Portuguese Convention of 1891 which stated that the boundary should follow the upper part of the eastern slope of Manica plateau southwards to the centre of the main channel to the confluence with Lundi River[19]. The Portuguese argued that the boundary

---

[19] Original Convention Document 'Anglo-Portuguese Convention of 1891' and Discussion minutes between Andrade and Jackson in 1891.

drawn by Major Leveson and reproduced in England was not in accordance with the treaty. Portugal argued that the boundary should follow Sabi River near Mutasa's kraal and follow southwards to the confluence with Lundi River. In other words, Portugal argued that Manica plateau (now Nyanga Mountains stretching to Vumba Ranges) lied in their territory of the now Mozambique.

Following the scramble for Africa, both natural and human resources were plundered and repatriated for the development of Europe. The practice also saw some wars of resistance being fought and in the process; thousands of people lost their lives. The colonization of Africa was also meant to create both markets for European products and a source for European industrial raw materials which were extracted at no payment. Zimbabwe was colonized by British South Africa Company (BSAC) whose board had been incorporated by the Royal Charter on 29 October 1889. Board members of the company which was headquartered at 15th Street Swithin Lane EC included the following; Duke of Abercorn K. G. (President), Earl Grey (Hon), Lord Gifford V. C. and George Cawston, Herbert Canning (Secretary), Jones J. F. (Assistant Secretary) and Clegg E. C. (Registrar).

The scramble for Africa, which gave the missionaries unlimited rights to preach their religion's gospel unfortunately allowed for the erosion of indigenous belief systems. It may be noted that as soon as the missionaries came to Africa, they weakened the local leaders by Christianizing them. In the process, indigenous traditions, cultures and spirits were pushed to the peri-phery. Closely related to the weakening of the traditional values was the land disempowerment by the same Europeans gradually pushing the indigenous people to the sandy soils in the agro-regions 3, 4 and 5 where rains were low and the climatic conditions not suitable for both habitation and agricultural production. Deliberately in 1903, the Europeans in Zimbabwe like everywhere else in Africa crafted a law to formalize the confiscation of the land from the indigenous people which was called the Reserve Act of 1903. It was this law which saw the creation of some of the earliest reserves like Gwaai, Shangani and Gokwe amongst others.

Boundary conflicts were also a daily phenomenon in most communities where the Europeans had established some settlements especially where they had forced local communities to relocate. As different communities were relocated, some ethnic groups were put together while some that could not share facilities were also forced to live together. Such arrangements were only a source of various fatal conflicts. Some of the boundary conflicts are still pronounced up till the 21st century.

Colonization of Africa though said to be bad had its share of positive developments. First and foremost, it allowed and perfected trade and commerce, which was necessary for both human and infrastructural development. The practice led to the establishment of formal trading systems and the industrialization of Africa. Development also requires cross-pollination of ideas. This is exactly what colonization helped to create after some indigenous people were taken to Europe before they returned some years later fostering development. Literacy in the modern sense was developed following the coming of Europeans who established schools and re-defined human rights and standard social practices. Most African rulers did not recognize standard social practices and human rights as they trusted no-one in their political systems. Therefore these leaders would kill arbitrarily recognizing no formal separation of powers.

The practice also led to an improved militarization of the defence systems. The Europeans who came to Africa brought with them arms of war and would either sell or give for free for use when repelling other Europeans seeking concessions with indigenous leaders. Europe is developed thus making life that side better and more enjoyable. Colonization of Africa opened up opportunities for Africans to go abroad for either studies or some other personal development. Ultimately, this brought civilization and development to individual household levels.

Improved health and educational services were brought into Africa following the coming of the European settlers in the 1820s. Prior to that era, Africans had their forms of social services which were somehow backward and dangerous to the health and wellbeing of the people. History has it that the rate of child mortality was high before the white settlers introduced the western forms of services. Lack of such services as formal education and schools also explains why Africa in general lagged behind in terms of development, research, education and health. It is not debatable that it was westernization of the local systems that established conditions for globalization that most 21st century societies do enjoy in various forms like entertainment, transportation, trade, food and clothing amongst others.

Like it has been rightly noted by Beach, the coming of Europeans into Zimbabwe changed the faces of many institutions including that of humanity. Beach points out that in 1920, Zimbabwe had 881 000 people and in 1992, the same country had a population of 10 400 000. Simply, this points to a variety of possibilities which ultimately cascade to the issue of the relevance of the European administration. Some of the possibilities are;

- Either the 1920 or 1992 population censuses were flawed. From simple arithmetic, if there was a population jump from 800 000 to 10 000 000 in 70 years, and another shift from 10 000 000 to 12 000 000 from 1992 to 2002, it means that in the first jump, there was a population growth of about 750 000 per year and yet in the second shift, there was a growth of 200 000 people per year. There are therefore two possibilities; either European administration was conducive for population growth or Zimbabwean administration was bad for population growth. This is against the background that population growth decreased after an indigenous administration had taken over in the 1980s. Below are some of the population growth statistics[20].

Fig 1.1 Population Growth Statistics

YR	AFRICANS	EUROPEANS	OTHER	TOTAL
1901	700 000	1100	1500	710 500
1905	770 000	1300	2100	790 000
1910	860 000	2100	---	880 000
1920	1 090 000	3 300	3 100	1 130 000
1930	1 380 000	4 800	4 100	1 430 000
1940	1 870 000	6 500	6 100	1 940 000
1950	2 600 000	12 500	9 700	2 730 000

---

[20] CSO (1976) CSO Supplement to the Monthly Digest of Statistics, Salisbury, October 1976.

| 1960 | 3 610 000 | 21 800 | 16 600 | 3 840 000 |
| 1970 | 5 050 000 | 23 900 | 25 300 | 5 310 000 |

- There was massive migration/immigration between the two censuses.

- Social services (health, education and sanitation) were improved that infant mortality rate decreased. This simply showed the importance of the Europeans into the Zimbabwean administration as it suddenly improved the social services. In 1891, Salisbury Sanitary Board attempted to relocate Salisbury Town from the present day Harare site to any of the following; Norton, Darwendale, Umvukwesi (Mvurwi) or Rusapi citing sanitation reasons. The argument was that the town had been sited upstream Hunyani River which flowed into the proposed site for Lake McLeweyn (now Lake Chivero) which was to supply the town with water.

- Other general deaths were reduced following the eradication/control of infectious diseases like smallpox, *trypanosomiasis* and malaria. European administration established several social facilities like schools and health centres where the generality of the people received attention.

- Food production and dietary conditions were improved that life expectancy went up. Europeans brought with them sophisticated efficient and effective machinery for agricultural production so much so that there was enough production for both local consumption and export. It subsequently benefitted the economy.

People were no longer expected to spend long hours working manually in the field thereby eating away their life spans.

- General lifestyle and entertainment were improved.

- The majority of indigenous people enjoyed peace of mind.

- Less than 500 European policies improved the lives of over 800 000 people.

Common Conflicts

Like any other society, the local communities also experienced conflicts which had varying effects and repercussions. Because the indigenous people occupied no clearly demarcated areas and because they got their livelihoods from common sources like pastures, rivers and wild fruits, they were bound to clash often. Actually most of their conflicts were over resource scarcity, ideological differences and criminal tendencies. Some of the recorded conflicts ranged from land disputes, grazing land, revenge attacks, cattle rustling, sexual harassment, adultery, murder, assault, arson, theft, witchcraft accusations, water rights, fishing and hunting rights, firewood, and harvesting wild fruits, to leadership and the desire to expand territories. There were also cases of house confiscation, trade disparities and non-payment of tributes which also led to fatal wars between communities.

Though most of the communities in the early kingdoms in Africa shared some relationships especially in the areas of trade and commerce, there were also instances when there were breakdowns of diplomatic relations often leading to inter-communal conflicts and violence. In the area of religion, there were also several instances when conflicts could be triggered either within families or in the entire communities. Such conflict triggers ranged from breaking of consecrated sanctions, insulting ancestors, violation of taboos, and abuse of shrines amongst others. Some of these conflicts resulted in violence sometimes fatal and bloody while others ended with the creation of new friendships and alliances.

My analysis of the Police diary[21] and particularly a report by Officer Commanding Mazoe Fort on 5 September 1896 shows that the natives who are referred to as 'niggers or kefirs' in the entire diary had had enough of fighting and beating by the Native Commissioner-led policemen and wanted to till land. Actually, to support the argument that the natives were being persecuted and oppressed on a daily basis are incidents of torture, livestock confiscation, arson, harassment and execution by the Europeans. Between 1 and 10 September 1896, the villages around the Granite Kopje were raided and burnt down on five different occasions by the European policemen on horses allegedly for various reasons; resistance to provide labour, conspiracy to attack the Europeans and other criminal accusations. Similarly, on 4 September 1896 at 0300hours Chief Makoni was captured by soldiers under Major Watts with Lieutenant Fischat effecting the arrest for allegedly leading an armed rebellion. He was tried by Field General Court Martial and sentenced to death. When Watts wired the High Commissioner for confirmation of the death sentence and getting no response following the escape of six other prisoners; Makoni's son, Chief's counselor '*jinda*' and an unidentified Headman, Watts went ahead executing Makoni by shooting him on the 4th of September midday of 1896. Interestingly, Watts was subsequently arrested on 9 September of the same year by the

[21] Original and unedited BSA Police daily diary at Mazoe Fort, now Mazowe Police station.

Order of the High Commissioner pending the assembly of a Court of Inquiry on his conduct in shooting a prisoner of war. During the same period in 1896 September, a Native Commissioner for Lo-Maghonda now Lomagundi called Campbell, *Kamswera* also went on a spree persecuting local natives; burning down their homes and confiscating their livestock. This to some extent contributed to an uprising by the natives in that area led by Mashayamombe, and Mapondera amongst others.

The uprisings were spontaneous in all the areas as the cruelty and ill-treatment of Africans by Europeans was almost similar and had reached alarming levels. To the east was Chief Makoni while around the central plateau were Kaguvi and Chaminuka[22] amongst others. The strength and determination in the uprisings were however watered down by the double-standards on the part of the other chiefs and traditional leaders who were also expected to fight alongside the African forces and yet collaborated with the Europeans. Some of the identified chiefs included; Chirimuhanzu who sided with Weale by providing with a police force in 1895, Chivi supported Belingwe Laager and also provided with 1800 soldiers for the attack of Mutekedza in August 1896[23], Ranga of Njanja (Kwenda) and Machedu Matibi collaborated with Brabant in 1896, and Hokonya refused to help Maromo and instead supported Cape Africans and made peace with Taylor while Zimuto and Makuvaza Gutu helped the Native Commissioner raise forces. Others were Chief Banga who joined hands with Forestall and Weale to help Hurrell attack Nhema in

---

[22] Kaguvi and Chaminuka were only spirit mediums for figures that had existed during the great trek into Chivavarira.

[23] Hist. MSS. WE3/2/6.

July 1896[24] and Kwenda who also raised a fighting force for the Europeans[25].

Conflict Dynamics

Conflicts are experienced differently and in varying degrees largely depending on the following; level of civilization, availability of resources, visibility of a solution, number of participants, duration of the conflict and the value of the issues at the centre of the conflict amongst others. Conflicts change over time and the nature of their dynamism also depends on the following; rate of development, level of participants' literacy, weaponry available, level of technology and the age ranges of the participants amongst others. The various factors outlined above have clearly brought to the fore two glaring variables; level of civilization and the rate of development. The two broad factors have indeed played a role in the nature of the conflicts that have been so far recorded in most parts of Africa. The level of development and civilization have also been to some extent affected by the era in which a particular people existed; the dark era, the dead era and the development era.

This section will not go into detail in respect of each of the variables outlined above. Suffice to highlight that in the early nation-states of Zimbabwe, various conflicts were recorded and all presented themselves in various shapes and scales thus making them distinctive and ungeneralizable. It was therefore the nature of a conflict which determined the approach that the parties and the mediators took to

---

[24] Hurrell to G.O.C, 2/8/96

[25] 7th Hussars Diary, 27/10/96.

address. However, it has to be noted that the approaches or mechanisms that were taken to address conflicts had a serious bearing on the conflict's fatalities and the period that each conflict took to resolve. There were other measures that required a lot of patience and time so much so that during the period, many lives and resources could be lost.

Conflict Effects

Closely akin to the above is that conflicts by their nature are expensive both materially and financially. It has to be known that conflicts are by nature also meant to instill fear, force an ideological shift, inflict pain and subject the other party to unpleasant conditions until he or she surrenders. While conflicts may not necessarily lead to violence, in most times, the pain and suffering that they cause is as bad as that caused by violence. It is therefore because of the nature and gravity of the conflict effects that we are sometimes forced to study conflict resolution measures.

Earlier on we talked about the phases that the earliest nation-states went through as they developed as; the '*dark era, the dead era* and the *development era*'. This has been disputed by other scholars who believe that it was the western education and colonialism which helped underdevelopment[26]. First was the '*dead era*', a period when people lived each day as it came without regard for the need for development and growth. History has out rightly failed to account for any of the

---

[26] Katola M. (2014) Incorporation of Traditional African Cultural Values in the Formal Education System for Development, Peace Building and Good Governance, *European Journal of Research in Social Sciences*, Vol. 2/3, P. 31-39

activities by the people who existed then. This period is as good as it never existed. There was also the '*dark era*'. During this period, people had not yet seen and embraced civilization and development which ultimately brought them to the present world of technology and at the pace that they have evolved and developed. However, the difference between this era and the '*dead era*' is that in the former, civilization was now on the door step and the willing few had already started assimilating some modern practices. The '*development era*' is the period when the Europeans had established systems for development and a mechanism had been put in place to ensure that civilization could be forced into the indigenous people. During this era which stretches from around the 1890s, laws were being put in place to force certain activities and developments to take place. This forced development ushered in the present development that Zimbabwe prides itself of. It is therefore because of the conflicts that were noted during the three phases that development and civilization were recorded in Zimbabwe.

Conflict Phases Identified

Looking at the period that has been reflected in this study; from the pre-documented times before the coming of westerners who saw the wisdom in archiving events to the late 1970s, the period of the liberation war, it has been established that various conflict resolution systems were employed. Different conflict situations and violent occasions were addressed using appropriate force and strategies depending on the availability of resources.

Endogenised diplomacy (till 1820s)

This was an era when the Ndebele and Shangani People were moving into the now Shona territory as they tried to either expand their spheres of influence or fled wars in their original areas. The local people then known as '*Marudzi*' had effective methods of resolving conflicts. Besides, they had a diplomatic way of receiving foreigners, which sought to avert potential conflicts. In this approach, they made use of all the available structures to persuade conflicting parties to make peace and respect the local spirits.

Inter-ethnic cleansing and extermination (1920s- 1850s)

Inter-ethnic cleansing and extermination was recorded from the period when the Ndebele people moved into the now Shona people's land. Naturally the Ndebele were jingoistic in nature having lived a fighting lifestyle under the Zulu kingdom and having fought all their way up to the Shona people's land. On the contrary, the Shona groups were peace-loving. It was only after the Ndebele had started to invade the Shona land confiscating livestock and women that the Shona groups decided to fight back leading to loses of lives especially within the latter ethnic groups. It

[27] Dodo O, E. Chikohora, A. Muzenje, G. Dodo & M. Zihanzu, (2017), Killing, Viewed from a Conflict Resolution Perspective: A 'Just Punishment' Using the Shona People's Lenses, *Mgbakoigba, Journal of African Studies*. 7(1), 1-13

was during this era that the most trusted and effective methods of resolving conflicts involved fighting and to some extent, eliminating conflict leaders[27].

The Europeans also seemed to enjoy the Shona-Ndebele conflicts as they allowed them an opportunity to move in and explore the natural resources. It also ensured that there would not be unity by the two ethnic groups against the interests of the Europeans. It also meant that the more the two groups fought, the more they eroded their cultural practices and belief systems, which served as their sources of strength and wisdom. It was good for the Europeans who wanted to sell their religious doctrines of Christianity and Islam.

Westernized conflicts (1850s-1890s)

There was a period when the Shona fought against the Ndebele. However, the two groups came to a point when they realised that their interests were being interfered by the Europeans. Soon, they sought to side with the third party as a way of securing sophisticated weapons. Realizing this, the Europeans then took advantage of the situation to further fuel the Shona-Ndebele conflicts. During this period, the conflicts were no longer so much about the Ndebele seeking to disempower the Shona economically. Rather, the conflicts were simply a creation by the Europeans who continually created hatred and hostility among the people. This helped the Europeans entrench their interests and solidify their position.

Identity crisis (1890s-1930s)

The hostility and enmity between the Ndebele and Shona that were created by the Europeans between the 1850s till the 1890s created two distinct groups of Africans across both the Ndebele and the Shona. These groups had been divided with some siding and seeking to identify with the Europeans' interests as a survival strategy while others were purely conservative. It was also the same period when the Europeans had introduced their religions thereby seriously pacifying the local cultures and practices.

The new religions had taught the indigenous people that local cultures and belief systems were satanic and evil. European form of education had also been introduced and everyone who was doing well attained some 'pseudo-European' status with all supporting material and social benefits. Besides, everyone who identified with the indigenous practices was seen with a suspicious lens and condemned as evil. Therefore, some people were beginning to join the new dispensation brought by the Europeans. This seriously created confusion within the indigenous people so much so that they could not identify with their original and indigenous systems. This period saw a serious identity crisis. It however has to be acknowledged that it was largely this identity crisis and European sponsored conflicts which brought in development and modernity among the indigenous people. It also has to realised that the new forms of conflict resolution that came on board fused indigenous and exogenous approaches thus creating endogenous systems; moving away from violence and adopting talks.

Intellectualized approach (1930s-1960s)

The coming of the Europeans especially their form of education, created a new people who appreciated negotiations ahead of violence and arrogance. The new crop of leadership that had acquired some western education preferred more peaceful and sustainable approaches to conflict resolution. It is important to highlight the fact that the most educated indigenous people dressed more like Europeans, work with Europeans and derived integrity from among the Europeans. These factors drove them to adopt a more civil and harmonious approach to conflict resolution.

Confrontational approach (1960s-1970s)

The phase of confrontational conflict resolution was recorded in the late 1950s into the 1970s following the refusal by the Europeans to extend full benefits to their fellow African who had attained almost the same status as the Europeans academically and professionally. While initially Europeans had promised to upgrade the status of every African who adopted their religion and acquired western education, when the numbers had swelled, the promise was abandoned. This was the beginning of a confrontational approach to conflict resolution.

The African had acquired enough western education and was now demanding full responsibility in spreading Christianity just like their fellow European priests. Similarly, the Africans were also demanding political recognition since they had also attained western education on leadership. During this phase, an ideal approach to conflict resolution demanded some confrontation.

Summary

Conflict resolution in Zimbabwe as has been discussed is a wide and complex practice which did develop over a long period of time. To the indigenous communities, it was a practice which served an important role while to the foreigners; it also helped in their assimilation into the communities. The chapter discussed the origins of the indigenous peoples of Zimbabwe tracing them back to the 'fairy' Guruuswa, looked at some of the methods used in resolving conflicts in those olden days and their merits and challenges thereto. The discussion presented an analysis of the population growth over the period juxtaposing to the presence of the Europeans. Because conflicts manifested variedly, there were also varied approaches to their resolutions. The discussion also looked at those areas. To clearly understand the development of politics in Zimbabwe pre-colonisation, we looked at the early states, their compositions, their developments and how they finally collapsed. Their collapse then led the discussion to the colonization of Zimbabwe and how the process of colonization impacted on the local people and their development.

CHAPTER TWO

PRE-ENLIGHTENMENT ERA CONFLICT RESOLUTION

Introduction

Before the colonial era in the now-Zimbabwe, people lived communally and precisely along ethnic and village lines for various reasons but chief amongst them for security reasons and to help mobilise resources as outlined in the Social Solidarity Theory by Emile Durkheim and Social Capital Theory by Putnam (1965). When talk about conflict resolution starts, the general impression that comes out is that the concept is new to the African arena and especially in Zimbabwe. What is rarely experienced in most of the developing countries is a deliberate effort towards researches that seek to lay the facts bare to the effect that indeed, Africa had since time immemorial practiced its effective community and culturally accepted conflict resolution approaches. These approaches were also supported by cultural and social values, customs and philosophies that were acceptable in the respective societies with reverence, transparency, participation, societal unity, coordination, peaceful co-existence, patience and self-effacement amongst others. These practices are now commonly termed 'endogenous conflict resolution'.

In other words, conflict resolution within the indigenous peoples dates back to the creation of mankind and perfected over the years. It is unfortunate that the early indigenous people did not document any of their practices in a standard and sustainable manner thus resulting in some of the data collected coming from oral and hearsay sources. However some of the activities and practices supported by some archeological artifacts and written accounts by the early Europeans have to some extent helped us to mobilise and document some of the conflict resolution practices that were practiced in the olden days. This chapter therefore looks at some of the practices that were common during the pre-enlightenment era.

Early Practices: An Introduction

During the pre-enlightenment era, which I will refer to as the 'dark age[iv]' , societies led by the elderly community had solid and effective mechanisms for resolving conflicts as explained in Chapter One. These mechanisms were to some extent supported by other social systems like traditional healers, spiritualists, herbalists, prophets, and mediums. In these societies, everyone from the eldest to the youngest had a responsibility towards maintaining peace and order. Given that traditionally every member in society had some cultural value, each enjoyed his/her position with regards to conflict and peace. At the end of the day, the essence of conflict resolution was to fix broken social relations, reestablish community order, execute cultural rites and offer reparations where necessary. The indigenous peoples had their own means of resolving conflicts for thousands of years before the coming of Europeans. It is these systems that are now referred to as endogenous systems. However, the coming of Europeans and some Arabs in the 14th century also saw the introduction of completely new conflict resolution systems which were sometimes not compatible with the local cultures and beliefs. These are what are now called exogenous systems of conflict resolution. Therefore, it is around the 14th century that the two systems of conflict resolution interacted before gradually merging into a compatible system. Over time, influenced by globalisation, literacy and modernity, exogenous system has eaten up the endogenous practices.

Conflict resolution during the pre-enlightenment era and through the pre-colonial era was done, facilitated and enhanced differently. Overall, it should be realized that the early efforts towards conflict resolution were largely conducted in the following broad ways; negotiation, mediation, arbitration, reconciliation and adjudication[28]. They all sought to achieve peace, order and harmony and that first and foremost required a high level of social and cultural etiquette, humanity, education about the cultural expectations and respect for each other.

The Practices

It may be necessary to briefly look at the above cited broad approaches before we delve into the other methods below. Negotiation was one of the approaches which relied on cooperation, compromise and consensus

---

[28] Braimah, A. (1968). "Culture and Tradition in Conflict Resolution", in Chris Garuba (ed.) *Capacity Building for crisis management in Africa.* Abuja: National War College.

among stakeholders for an effective outcome. In the traditional African conflict resolution domain, negotiation also involved the spirit world's intervention besides drawing a lot of support from the elderly community who were full of wisdom in both communication persuasion and compromise[29]. The fact that some early societies agreed to the involvement of a third party in their conflicts showed the importance of mediation in the traditional conflict resolution processes. It to some extent showed the following aspects; that conflicting parties would have been tired of conflicting and now frustrated, restoration of sensibility in the parties and trust in the mediators, fear of losing their integrity in public, some belief that the process could produce a sustainable outcome and a sense of allowing social justice and progress[30]. This practice involved everyone in society from passers-by to close relatives who had the capacity to simply intercede in a conflict especially when parties engaged in physical fighting. It did not only involve quenching a conflict, but restoring friendly relationships.

Arbitration is pronouncedly an exceptional way of identifying an arbitrator who made crucial decisions which the parties to the conflict were expected to submit themselves to. Arbitration as a process had produced high levels of confidence, hope and mutual understanding in the local societies as it depended on the injunctions of the supernatural and tradition[31]. Truthfulness, flexibility and non-formality to the arbitrage often made the verdicts of the arbitrators easily acceptable and

---

[29] See Braimah

[30] Ojielo, M.O (2001). Alternative Dispute Resolution (ADR) Lagos: Centre for Peace in Africa.

[31] Allott, A.N. (1960). Essays in African Law London: Butter-Worths.

valuable in local societies. Adjudication has remained one of the powerful resources of cultural heritage in as far as conflict resolution is concerned. Judgment in traditional adjudication processes did not seek to identify the perpetrator or loser or punish but to restore peace and harmony and promoting *'esprit de corps'*. As a process, adjudication had an exceptional capacity to identify the right or wrong side in conflict issues, an assignment that demanded great intellects, functional recollection, rapid reaction and impartial listing of thorny issues. It has to be pointed out that effective adjudication traditionally involved rapt attention, tactfully paying attention and maximum thought application of the practices and standards of the society.

Conflicts by their nature disrupt peace, tranquility and order. They break relationships and create animosity amongst people. Therefore, the early African societies in general and the Zimbabwean in particular had reconciliation as a relationship restoration measure in place. The process was created to calm down the parties in conflict without subverting the social order and cultural growth. In conflict phraseology reconciliation implies a means of attaining a pact or concession in the direction of curing the wounds of conflict. Reconciliation traditionally established a channel through which community members could forward their thought pattern on the area of common understanding thereby oiling the apparatus of social development epitomized in African cultural heritage. The process acknowledged the subtleties of pacification and the comforting of the provoked players in the conflict. Traditionally, pacification and coaxing circled around the knowhow and previous familiarity of the pacificator, who, as a third party was full of strength and energy to restore peace and harmony back to the society[32].

In the early societies in Zimbabwe, reconciliation allowed for humane conduct and the maintenance of ideal morality and social harmony which enabled sociability and friendliness[33]. The fact that early societies in Zimbabwe lived communally, meant that they could not do without the other. What it therefore meant was that whenever they had conflicts, they needed to quickly restore their relationships through whatever means but at the end of it all, needed to reconcile so they could move on again as a collective.

On 11 September 1896, Lieutenant French supported by 20 soldiers and an interpreter called Sam Khosa met some of the chiefs under the Hwata area at Dandamira hills for a peaceful settlement to the hostilities that had developed between the two communities. Some of the chiefs who attended the meeting included: Maswi, Chidamba, Shiwishi, Shitawaro, Kamutaka, Deve, Gwanzura, Shewanga, Matatawana and an unidentified brother to Hwata. Hwata and Garande were hiding in the mountains as they feared arrest for allegedly inciting their subjects to resist Native Commissioners' oppressive tendencies. During the meeting, the chiefs indicated that they had been influenced by the Ndebele to rise against the Europeans before they apologized to French. As a gesture of peace and good neighbourliness, the chiefs offered some goats to the Mazoe Fort and indicated that they could not offer cattle as most of their cattle had been confiscated by the raiding Ndebele a few weeks before.

---

[32] Driberg, J.H. (1934). The African Conception of Law, *Journal of African Society,* 34, Supplement, July.

Norbeck, E. (1963). African Rituals of conflict, *American Anthropologist,* 65 (6).

[33] Smock, David R, and Crocker, C.A. (eds.) (1995). African Conflict Resolution, Washington: US Institute of Peace.

What is important to realize is that, the indigenous peoples have a rich cultural heritage which boasts of the following amongst others; strict recognition and adherence to the marriage rites, adherence to social and cultural rites like *bira* (ancestral dance ceremonies), *kuripa* (compensation), *kurova guva* (appeasement of the dead), *roora* (marriage), and *rufu* (death)[34]. The early indigenous people believed that proper adherence to these and several other rites helped to build cordial relations with both the ancestors and the living 'others'. Though the processes that were followed during the rituals were not written for consistency, the elderly leaders could still follow the expected procedures and this helped to nurture the relationships in society.

During the pre-enlightenment era, the nature of conflicts that were experienced are slightly different from those experienced in the contemporary era to some extent due to the effects of globalization, literacy, breakdown in social relationships and boundaries, the nature and value of the valuables that people own, the type of governance system, and to some extent, the weaponry used during conflicts. The main forms of conflict resolution that were practiced mainly employed the use of human skills and in some cases the use of medicine and livestock. To conduct and facilitate the talks and other forums that helped resolve conflicts, various people would be employed for their noted skills that ranged from persuasion, talking, arguing to patience and perseverance amongst others. In conflict resolution, medicine was used for various purposes; to influence the behaviours or decision of another, to calm a potentially volatile situation, to heal the injured or hurt and to kill if need

[34] Some of these cultural rituals are explained in Dodo O. (2015) Endogenous Conflict Resolution Approaches: The Zezuru Perspective. IDA, Harare

be amongst others while livestock was used to compensate the victims or as food during special ceremonies amongst others.

Conflict resolution that was common during the pre-enlightenment era was largely guided by the spirit mediums and soothsayers and to some extent by the community elders who would then consult with their village councils and spouses. There was a belief in those communities that the dead had some powers to oversee what was happening in the families and villages from wherever they were living. The power of the ancestral spirits and the dead could also be seen when the former dictated pace on how life could be lived. It must be realized that with the coming of the Europeans, there was massive development and industrialization which required people to work and be able to pay their taxes. In defiance, beginning 1912-13, traditional leaders commandeered the observance of the holy day commonly called *'chisi'*, stop selling their grain and stop purchasing of foreign tradable goods. This was specifically meant to improve their relationships with the dead. There was also another belief that the spirits of the dead could liaise with those of another family. Actually, the belief suggested that the dead had their own community somewhere where they could talk and share ideas. This therefore meant that the ancestral spirits of the feuding families could help pacify an earthly conflict and relay the position through the spirit mediums. In Matebeleland area at Empandeni, an elderly priestess called Ninakapansi (Mother of the ground) censured members of the rural elite for failing to propitiate God (*Mwari*). She claimed to have communicated with God before her action.

Natural phenomenon like winds, rains, droughts, floods, veld fires, lightning and other natural disasters were also used to interpret decisions that were believed to have been made by the dead either fighting for or in defence of their living relatives. Whenever such natural events were recorded, community leaders would then consult with the spirit mediums for possible clues and solutions before they were advised to conduct traditional rituals. There were various forms of traditional rituals that were conducted in the early societies of the now-Zimbabwe. These ranged from the appeasement of the dead (*kurova guva*), spiritual dance ceremony (*bira*) and compensating the avenging spirits (*kuripa ngozi*)[35]. These rituals amongst others served to pacify anger and hostility amongst community members, revitalize relationships with the ancestral spirits, appease the spirits of the other parties in a conflict, compensate the aggrieved families and their dead's spirits, acknowledge the good facilitated by the ancestors and to maintain good relations with the gods.

It is acknowledged that indigenous traditional societies had fewer cases of conflicts as compared to the 21st century Africa. According to some scholars, it was because individual interests were subservient to those of the community and that the core curriculum were full of peace education[36]

[35] See Dodo O. (2015), (p. 3, 33, 75)

[36] Boulding, E (2001) Peace Culture and Social Action. *Peace Review* Vol. 13/4 p.67-70.

Bujo, B (1998) The Ethical Dimension of Community. The African Model of Dialogue between North and South. Nairobi: Pauline Publications Africa.

Gyekye, K (1996) African Cultural Values. An Introduction. Philadelphia: Sankofa Publishing Company.

[37] Dodo O. (2015) Traditional Taboos Defined: Conflict Prevention Myths and Realities. IDA, Harare.

unlike the contemporary curricula which focuses on individualization of interests and the promotion of power and military might. In the olden days, peace education was to some extent pushed through the use of taboos[37] which instilled fear in children so much so that they refrained from engaging in immoral and socially unacceptable activities. Taboos also helped in the control and preservation of natural resources, condemnation of some social practices like incest, murder, rape and theft and the development of human skills and capacities.

Closely akin to the above is the issue about human relationships which were also promoted through early forms of education. In the early social settings, human relationships fostered the idea of extended families and the importance of respect in relationships. To a great extent, this enhanced community welfare support which subsequently led to a reduction in social conflicts. To some extent, human relationships emphasised on the power of the almighty and the other gods. This recognition and respect of the supernatural spirits and gods helped control the behaviours of the people.

The history of conflict resolution in the pre-colonial now-Zimbabwe is described in various forms. Following various cases of conflicts within the states especially amongst the leadership and some members of the royal family, some wise people thought about some measures that could help address the conflicts. By the 14th century, political centralization had been started by Mutota, a strategy that allowed him to conquer the Korekore and Tavara of the Dande and Chidema areas respectively. Political centralization was a strategy whereby all the state power could be entrusted into the hands of a king and a few trusted members of the royal family. The strategy primarily ensured that no other centre of power could be created thus leading to conflicts over power. For a very long time, the strategy worked so much so that the Mutota state expanded till he was given a title '*Mwene Mutapa*'.

To further strengthen the conflict resolution systems, the Mutota King brought together religion and politics. This practice of intertwining religion and politics meant that he as the King would be in control of the soothsayers, dreamers and spirit mediums that had the power to foretell the future. Besides, the practice was also meant to scare away all potential threats through the use of religious taboos and belief systems. Most of these early states survived on the advice of the spirit mediums of the likes of Mbuya Nehanda, Sekuru Chaminuka and Sekuru Kaguvi amongst others. What should however be noted here is that when the Europeans entered these early states, they first and foremost established the local leaders' sources of power before they penetrated the systems and weakened from within. What they established was that the local leaders derived their power from their traditional religion especially the spirit mediums. In no time, most of them had been baptized into Christianity. Besides using European religion to weaken the indigenous conflict resolution systems, western education was also roped in to both brainwash and enlighten the communities on the good of modernity. This marked the beginning of the collapse of the traditional conflict resolution and prevention systems.

Abandonment and avoidance are some of the historically documented practices by the early states and which served as effective conflict resolution and preventive systems. There was a belief that if there was a conflict and one party believed that its prospects of winning were slim, one of the best options was to simply run away to a far-away place.

Besides saving the embarrassment of having suffered a clear defeat, it allowed the 'coward' to start a new life and possibly avail an opportunity to create a new kingdom. Beach[38] in his historical accounts tells us that the Great Zimbabwe state collapsed after the leadership had abandoned it and fled while in the south-western part, Nkulumane[39], an acting King in the Mzilikazi kingdom also fled upon hearing that the substantive King had come for his throne and also wanted to kill him. Instead of waiting for a fight, which apparently would have brought a clear defeat, the weaker parties simply fled.

The world-over, since time immemorial, violence and fighting have been some of the most effective and sustainable means for resolving conflicts. In these early states, these two mechanisms were also valuable in that regard. Whenever parties failed to resolve conflicts through some of the available peaceful means, fighting usually became the last resort especially after the coming in of the guns with the foreign traders. During the 1660s, Mukombwe rebelled against his leadership before he went on to chase away the Portuguese missionaries and traders between 1664 and 1704. After chasing away the Portuguese, the King resettled his people on the farms that had been occupied by the former. That way, the King managed to strengthen his relationship with his subjects through the availability of the land resource. During the 1880s, there was also another rebellion against Mutapa Mukombwe by Changamire Dombo[40]. Again, the 1896/7 Matabeleland and Mashonaland uprisings against the BSAC must have send some messages to the participants with regards to

---

[38] Ibid

[39] See Ranger

[40] See Samkange

the effects of fighting following the death and injury of 451 and 188 Europeans[41] respectively while indigenous Africans lost an estimated six thousand people. All these incidents clearly show the existence of a conflict otherwise that could not be resolved peacefully and that might have existed for ages without prospects to an end. Therefore, the insurgents' actions could have been invaluable given the circumstances.

Some conflicts and potentially volatile situations were addressed through concessions. There were instances when different parties could enter into agreements of compromise as a way of averting hostilities and violence. There were also cases when a conflict or war conqueror could then dictate the terms of operations and or relationships to his or her advantage. Such was the type of concession that was made between the Ndebele state leadership and the London Missionary Society through Robert Moffat subsequently leading to the establishment of a mission station at Inyati in 1852.

Polygyny and polygamy are family types that are common the world-over especially within the African set-up. The former involves a man married to more than two wives while the latter is when a woman is married to more than two men. The latter in most African cultures is a bit unusual and taboo. What is however common is the monogamy type of family where a man marries a single woman. But polyandry and monogamy have worked and still work effectively and peacefully.

Marriage has traditionally been used as a conflict resolution measure but in this discussion, I wish to make reference to the type of family as the critical component in the resolution of conflicts. Generally in an African

---

[41] The 1896 Rebellions. BSAC Reports on the Native Disturbances in Rhodesia, 1896-1897, Vol. 2 (1975), Books of Rhodesia Pub, Bulawayo.

set-up, a family is made up of the father, mother, children and the extended family. If a man is married to one wife, it means that the extended family is not so much 'extended' unlike that of a man who has several wives. Therefore, the coming together of several in-laws as a result of a marriage to one man is to some extent taken as a way of building relations. In the African system and the Zimbabwean early states in particular, the concept of relationship building was very important in controlling, preventing and resolving conflicts. The following presentation illustrates the nature of relationships that exist between and amongst people who are cross-married. Some of the relationships appear distant but do have value in the traditional circles and in maintaining relationships between individuals and communities.

Fig. 2.1 Cross-Relationships

NATURE OF RELATIONSHIP	RELATIONSHIP TO A MALE	RELATIONSHIP TO A FEMALE
Wife to a brother (*Mukadzi wemukoma*)	Wife (*Muramu*)/Husband (*Muramu*)	Aunt (*Maiguru*)/Aunt (*Tete*)
Wife to my wife's brother (*Mukadzi wehanzvadzi yemudzimai*)	In-law (*Ambuya*)/In-law (*Mukuwasha*)	In-law (*Ambuya*)/In-law (*Tete*)
Brother to my wife (*Hanzvadzi yemudzimai*)	In-law (*Tezvara*)/In-law (*Mukuwasha*)	In-law (*Tezvara*)/In-law (*Mukuwasha*)
Mother's aunt (*Tete vamai*)	Aunt (*Amaiguru*)/Son (*Mwana*)	Aunt (*Amaiguru*)/Daughter (*Mwana*)
Husband to mother's aunt (*Murume watete vamai*)	Uncle (*Babamukuru*)/Son (*Mwana*)	Uncle (*Babamukuru*)/Daughter (*Mwana*)
Son to my mother's brother (*Mwana mukomana wehanzvadzi yamai*)	Uncle (*Sekuru*)/Nephew (*Muzukuru*)	Uncle (*Sekuru*)/Niece (*Muzukuru*)
Daughter to my mother's brother (*Mwana musikana wehanzvadzi yamai*)	Aunt (*Mainini*)/Son (*Mwana*)	Aunt (*Mainini*)/Daughter (*Mwana*)
Husband to your divorced wife (*Murume wemukadzi wawakarambana naye*)	Uncle (*Babamudiki*)/Uncle (*Babamukuru*)	Brother (*Hanzvadzi*)/Sister/Aunt (*Hanzvadzi/Tete*)
Friend's wife (*Mukadzi	Aunt (*Mainini/maiguru*)/	Aunt (*Muroora*)/ Aunt (*Tete*)

wasahwira)	Uncle (*Babamukuru/ babamudiki*)	

This brings me to the issue about totems which most Africans do use for identification. While totems were used as a conservation mechanism, they also helped in the identification of a people. Having identified a group of people, it meant that they were all closely related even if they did not know each other. It also meant that people of the same totem could not be expected to fight but to support each other. The concept meant that people of the same totem could not eat or use the animal, bird or part of that creature as it was considered sacred and attracting a harsh penalty socially and culturally. In some circles, it was believed that besides serving as a conservation mechanism, it created peace between humanity and the wildlife and equally between the people of a particular totem who did not eat or use that creature and the other groups that consumed.

Most communities had particular forms of cultural heritage; both tangible and intangible which they valued and protected from external influence and destruction. What defined a particular form of heritage was its relevance to most members of that community, the historical role that might have been played by that element, monument or artifact, and the cultural value that a particular community attaches to it. Some of the forms of cultural heritage include the following; sacred sites and natural establishments, craftsmanship, oral expressions, songs and traditions, including social practices, language, performing arts, knowledge and practices about natural surroundings and the cosmos and traditional stories[42]. Shrines and sites are part of the society and do play an important role in the social praxis. Therefore, if a particular community values a particular site or artifact for whatever reason, there is likelihood for collectivity in the event that there is a potential intruder or destruction. It is that collectivity that brought some communities together thus preventing the occurrence of some conflicts.

Community practices that were led by the local traditional leaders also played an important role in fostering peace and resolution of conflicts in most societies. In the olden days, traditional leaders had various community activities which helped them bring their subjects together. *Zunde Ramambo* and *Mukwerera* were some of them. These practices were a sacred and vital concept which the leaders used to either address the welfare of their people or glue the people together.

Zunde Ramambo was a communal cropping project that was administered by a Chief to produce food either for the strategic reserves or for the need members of the community such as the orphans, widows or the elderly. The production and management brought all the members of a particular community together thus unifying their relations. Similarly, the *Mukwerera* practice was a ritual led by traditional leaders and spirit mediums meant to ask the gods for rains. It was an equivalence of the present day cloud seeding. The rituals also required all the community members to work together and it also cemented the relations amongst the people.

The early societies also made use of extrajudicial measures as effective conflict resolution systems which were applied through approaches

---

[42] Munjeri, D. (1995). Spirit of the People, Nerve of Heritage. Paper Presented at the World Heritage Centre (WHC)/International Council of Monuments and Sites (ICOMOS) Meeting, Harare. 11-15 October 1995

measured metaphysical in style and application. According to these early people, it was God alone identified as the Supreme Being who had the power to put into effect decent morals of both the spiritual and earthly cosmoses. In the final analysis, the Supreme Being through unseen powers enhanced social stability and pleasant relationships in communities. They were important builders of peace through the unseen command and inculcated emotional fear in the people. Oath-taking was one conflict resolution approaches under extrajudicial measures. Oath taking was used as a means for finding amends of breaches of the social rules, to determine guilt among the suspects and to identify adultery and witchcraft practitioners in the community[43]. The power of oaths was derived from the belief that the ancestors had the power to afflict or plague fellow members of the community with either sickness or other calamities until one either confessed or apologized appropriately.

Education during the Dark Age

In this section, we want to understand how people in the 'Dark age' acquired knowledge and got educated on various other issues. In this discussion, education refers to the means by which relevant and important information could be transmitted to other people for either immediate use or for future dissemination. In other words, knowledge could be transmitted through socialisation rather than the modern day classroom pedagogy. It was from this constituency of the 'educated' that intellectuals could be developed and who could also help in sharpening conflict resolution skills.

[43] Ayisi, E.O. (1979). An Introduction to the study of African culture (2nd ed.) London: Heinemann Educational Books

Well before the coming of civilization courtesy of the Europeans into Africa and Zimbabwe in particular, all indigenous communities had their ways of educating each other. There were different syllabi for different ethnic groups, age groups and sexes and all followed a somewhat informal system. There were no set times for education nor set institutions but knowledge and knowledge masters in the form of elderly and wise members of either the families or the communities. Some experienced wise members would become so knowledgeable that they were consulted by other groups.

The curriculum for the early education system covered amongst others the following pertinent areas; obedience, uprightness, reverence, and kindness. Learning through socialisation could be enhanced through participation where children would take part in a practice or rite and in the process acquire the relevant skills. This was prevalent in such practices like slaughtering a beast '*kuuraya mombe*', construction of a house '*kuvaka imba*' or physical fighting '*kurwa*'. In other cases, some people could be allowed to partake in some activity thus allowing them an opportunity to see how it was done. Without really doing it, they could over time acquire the skills and knowledge. Appeasement of the spirit of the dead '*kurova guva*' is a ritual which is a preserve of the village elders. However, as the elders conduct the ceremony, the young ones see and acquire the skills so much so that they are able to apply them on their own. Traditionally, most households had a sitting place outside of the hut where men would sit at night '*dare*' telling stories and discussing other family matters. It was during the 'dare' time that young people learnt about their historical backgrounds and about bravery through stories and other folk-tales. In rare instances, girls and boys in their teens could be taken separately for manhood and womanhood initiation by the uncles and aunts. This initiation process allowed participants to sit before a teacher who would give some lectures on sexual and romantic matters before some practical could be conducted. This was a way of preparing the youngsters for their lives in marriages. There were also rare instances when young people were denied the chance to learn normally and would either eavesdrop or peep as adults engaged in the acts. Such cases were rampant in some sexual antics like romance and sexual intercourse positions which might not have been covered during the initiation ceremonies.

What I note in this early form of education by the indigenous peoples of Africa in general and the then pre-colonial Zimbabwe in particular is that the indigenous system sought to satisfy real learning, originality and resourcefulness in a manner that allowed the recipients to be able to make use of the acquired skills in real life situations. This is unlike the modern western type of education where recipients seek knowledge for examination purpose only and nothing beyond. The indigenous learning system also allowed the identification of productive talents within people and sought to sharpen for the benefit of the entire community. These talents though used commercially, benefited the local communities first. Closely akin to the above is that the form of education offered did not allow people to leave their areas for more profitable regions as in migration for economic purposes. Communities were closed and communal in nature that people did not see profit more than they saw community assistance. What is important to realize is that most prominently, the education system inculcated some spirit of self-identity; where people chose to identify themselves first with their relatives by way of totems and other variables like communities lived, resources shared like pastures and water points amongst others and extended relationships by way of distant marriages.

Another valuable point to take note in the indigenous education system is that, it was designed and imparted in a manner that promoted self-reliance. If a man was taught to engage in crop farming, he would be seen surviving on that activity. It emphasised on integrity and how a person presented him/herself to the outside world and this reflected on the entire family, clan and even the ancestral lineage. The education system focused on producing a dedicated and specialized graduate[44]. To a great extent, it reflected the type of teachers and their determination to impart real and sustainable knowledge. Peace and societal order was one of the intentions of the knowledge dissemination effort in the early days. There was an understanding that a well provided for community and well informed society engaged not in conflicts. There was also another understanding that a constantly communicating society and an always interacting community never misconceived or misperceived one another. This was pushed through some of the societal practices like communal task-work *'jakwara'* and routine village meetings. Like it has been noted[45], in these communities, peace education was imparted from childhood till adulthood so that people could appreciate and embrace the need for peace and order. Peace education was introduced variedly; through social etiquette, respect and worship of the God and ancestors and morality primarily to guard against state sponsored violence, liberative violence,

---

[44] Mugambi, J.N.K. (2003) "Principles and Traditions of Peace Making in Africa in Getui, M and Musyoni, W, M *Overcoming Violence.* Nairobi:NCCK

[45] Boulding E. (2001) Peace Culture and Social Action. *Peace Review,* 13/4 p.67- 570.

structural violence, physical violence, ecological violence and political violence[46].

It has to be noted that as people learnt various skills, it opened opportunities for democracy, good leadership and governance. These were provided for through respect of human rights (whatever they were then), establishment of the rule of law, transparency and accountability, dependability political openness and tolerance, and unfettered participation[47]. These principles were clear in the daily lives as people could recall their leaders from office in cases they failed to deliver. In reciprocity, the leaders also ensured that they went back to the people for consultations and feedback whenever need arose. Also prioritized in the education system then was the question of cooperation, sharing and oneness. This virtue was also imparted from birth till one reached old age.

Processes Followed

Conflict resolution, just like other practices like medicine and engineering has been an applied field. It needed a critical analysis in the form of a systematic conflict analysis before an appropriate solution was applied[48]. The processes of conflict resolution were conducted in various

[46] Rusatsi, A.F (2001) Ethnic Conflict in Africa and Reconciliation. In Ryan, P (Ed) *Ethnocentricism and Ethnic conflicts in Africa.* Nairobi: CUEA

[47] Kinoti, G (1994) Hope for Africa: And What the Christian Can Do. Nairobi: African Institute for Scientific Research and Development.

[48] Ojielo, M.O (2001). Alternative Dispute Resolution (ADR) Lagos: Centre for Peace in Africa.

ways; sitting together for talks, mediation, negotiation, and arbitration; all seeking to bring restorative justice as aptly pointed out in the Optimal Psychology Theory by Myers[49]. The processes were neither confrontational nor adversarial in nature; they sought to build sustainable relationships based on the fact that people shared various resources; water holes, pastures and land and they were somehow connected through the totems. Then, the practice worked well and effectively till the advent of westernized approaches which demonized all indigenous systems. What should be realized in the two practices; indigenous and western is that both followed almost similar concepts except that the latter were more advanced and polished and that they all believed in the concepts of acknowledgement before forgiveness if conflicts were to be sustainably resolved.

The processes of conflict resolution during the pre-colonial era were conducted variedly. The first type could be conducted at an open space where the elderly men sat at night called '*dare*' while the other could be in the hut in which women could be involved in the decision making process. Both processes could be either formal or informal depending on how the matter would have been introduced for discussion and the gravity of the case. Secondly, cases could be discussed in a chief's court and presided by the chief and supported by a council. There were also instances when people could discuss issues informally during a beer drink called '*ndari*'[50]. The last of the approaches was when an issue

[49] Myers L. J, (1992) Understanding an Afrocentric World View: Introduction to an Optimal Psychology, Kendall/Hunt.

[50] Dodo O, Ndanga E and Dodo G. (2012) Socio-Recreational and Disputes Resolution Values of Native Alcoholic Beers in Chikomba District, Zimbabwe. *African Journal of Social Sciences* Vol. 2/2 p.89-99

could be discussed in the bedroom between a husband and wife. The matter varied from being a family issue to a community one. If it was a community issue, then women could raise the issue with their husbands who sat in the Chief's Council as a way of influencing the outcome.

In all the approaches, what was clear and common was the aspect of tolerance, consultation in one way or the other and cooperation and that the processes were systematic and systemic in nature. Since the leadership believed that conflicts were inevitable in society, they were patient when dealing with the parties to conflicts. The elders also strongly believed in seeking outsiders' opinions before they passed final verdicts. Like I did indicate above, no matter the region or culture, the processes followed when resolving conflicts were almost similar and indeed followed a particular format which could then be passed from one generation to the other. Strict adherence to a format was associated with the unforeseen involvement of the ancestors who were believed to be a key player in the successes recorded in resolving conflicts and maintenance of peace and order in society. This is explained by the constant reference and presentation of the agenda to the clan or ethnic spirits for support and guidance at the start and end of the processes. It must also be noted that when the elders made reference and presented the agenda to the ancestors, they would be asking for a peaceful and sustainable resolution to a conflict. This comes against a background where it was traditionally believed that ancestors were peaceful, tolerant and forgiving.

Early Practitioners

Like it has been mentioned above, conflict resolution has been part and parcel of the Zimbabweans even well before colonialism and the coming of the Ndebele people in the 1830s. The practice meant to restore broken relations and to nurture peace and order in society was conducted by various personalities and groups in society. These early societies acknowledged the various capacities and potentials by each member in the community so much so that they eventually worked as a collective if they wanted to resolve a conflict. Each societal member played a distinct role towards the resolution of a conflict. This meant that even young children served as messengers, young girls serving as assistants in the preparation of food for negotiators, while women doubled as food caterers and also as part of the negotiating teams. It has to be realized that each of the parties in this puzzle had his/her way of seeing conflicts and how same could be resolved peacefully or otherwise as there were various approaches to conflict resolution. Impartiality, equity, fairness, transparency, justice and neutrality were the key principles that guided all the stakeholders in this process.

The local people strongly believed in fighting as a conflict resolution measure. It must be noted that from 1826 when the *Mfecane* revolution south of the Limpopo was experienced, several groups moved into the local states thus creating more conflicts. The most noted of them all was the Mzilikazi/Lobengula invasion of the Rozvi state. The local leaders then resorted to the use of the guns that were being availed by the foreign traders to fight back the Ndebele invasion. Manuel Antonio de Sousa *Guveya* also availed some guns to Hwata in 1875[51]. In 1889, a Portuguese called Andrade availed thousands of arms to several local

---

[51] See Beach (1995)

leaders so that they could defend themselves in times of aggression. Though there was a belief that he was sponsoring conflicts so that he could plunder the resources during the time they were fighting, to the local chiefs, the arms were handy defense-wise. Andrade gave thousands of guns to Chief Makoni[52] who was a sworn rival of Chief Mutasa. Almost during the same period, British South Africa Company (BSAC) gave blankets, rifles and ammunition to the same local leaders. Some of the Chiefs who benefitted from this 1890 BSAC donation[53] were Gomani, a tributary of Mutasa who got ten rifles and Mutasa who got fourteen rifles. Fighting eventually proved to be a very effective and efficient way of attending to the conflicts that were being imported by 'foreign' invaders. This clearly shows how some of the most local lethal weapons were introduced in local conflicts and respective conflict resolution systems. Following the invasion of the Shona territory by the Ndebele, there was an increasing level of violence mentality within the Shona people who were now paying more attention to raiding and warfare to make a living. In the 1880s, following an aggression by Francisco Barreto, a Portuguese expeditor, the King of the Uteve kingdom fought ruthlessly as a way of permanently resolving the conflict. Though we earlier on alluded to the fact that the Shona people were a peace loving community who saw fighting as a last resort, there were however instances when they proved that fighting was indeed an effective and efficient means through which conflicts could be addressed.

---

[52] Bhila, Hoyini H. K. (1982) *Studies in Zimbabwean History: Trade and Politics in the Shona Kingdom. The Manyika and their Portuguese and African Neighbours, 1575-1902*, Longman, UK.

[53] From an original and unedited diary of the BSA Police at Mazoe Fort.

In 1880, Chief Mutoko did send over 5000 soldiers under Gurupira, his son to help Chief Mutasa, a neighbour fight Manuel Antonio de Souza[54].

Like I did mention above, conflicts usually involve few members of the society but unfortunately affect almost every member in the same society. Therefore, realizing this danger, early societies would mobilise human resources from across the divide for a quick collective resolution. Whenever there were conflicts in society large-scale or small-scale, community elders would first and foremost assess the damage that might have been caused by that conflict before they sought a possible resolution mechanism. Finding the best resolution meant that there needed to be some consultation with the rest of the community elders and the spirit mediums who would also liaise with the ancestors. This process was long as it strictly followed cultural routines. Armed with a possible strategy whether to conduct a cultural ritual or ordinary talks, the elders then informed the traditional leaders who then devised a means of inviting all the stakeholders for consultative elementary programmes. In the case of ordinary talks, elderly women would then mobilise resources to feed all the participants during the talks. However, this was done in consultation with the family heads that apparently were the fathers and also part of the top most team. After agreeing on the possible meeting dates, the elders would assign the youths to move around spreading the dates and the invites.

As the meeting dates neared, the traditional leaders continued to consult spirit mediums for further advice and guidance. Similarly, the youth would also continue helping women with the logistical preparations; collection of firewood, water and security arrangements where necessary.

---

[54] See Bhila (1982)

The youth were also employed as intelligence gatherers ahead of any talks.

In the case of conducting cultural rituals, almost a similar procedure in the allocation of responsibilities was followed except that there was more involvement of the spirit mediums who liaised with the gods. Besides some of the food that was mobilised from the community, the chief or local traditional leaders also availed some resources like beasts and grain especially from the Chief's Granary (*Zunde Ramambo*). Traditionally, the Chief's Granary mobilised its resources from the chief's communal field and some of the beasts paid as fines to the chief's court.

Traditional Institutions of Conflict resolution

Conflict resolution in the pre-colonial Zimbabwe era existed in various forms. Each of the forms had its distinctive advantages and weaknesses which on the whole helped to nurture peace in most communities. This is against a background of a jingoistic society where power and politics were largely about killing each other and subjecting each other under one's authority. It is therefore prudent that we talk about some of the traditional institutions that were employed to sow and foster peace on the ground. Traditional institutions of conflict resolution are olden political arrangements that were in place and usually blessed by the ancestral powers and culturally acceptable to the communities to attend to issues about hostilities, enmity, wars and hatred amongst others. These institutions also made use of various systems to achieve their goals. Because most of these traditional institutions; the traditional court, the elderly and children, dare, public shrines, names and songs and the marriage institution amongst others have been discussed in detail by Dodo (2015)[55], they will not be discussed in detail but simply listed.

While this discussion will not delve deeper into this area, it is important that I highlight the fact that these traditional conflict resolution institutions were broadly categorised into the following; social (age-structures and professional groups), political (family and the Chief), and religious (ancestors, deities, and sanctuaries) and economic (market). The institutions often created an environment that allowed people to appreciate and read the customs which built peace, order and stability, and allowed an ideal sense of belonging and social responsibility which the individual owed the society and the need for an environment which allowed development and harmonious settlement to thrive. They also believed that sustainable resolutions were based on the following; accomplishment of objectivity and the improvement of transparency and compromise, confidence of the followers, demonstration of impartiality and social justice, confirmation of actuality, as well as observance to clemency and lenience. Finally, I need to point out that it was almost compulsory for members of the community to know about each of the traditional institutions as they were regarded custodians of '*de facto*' constitutions.

Ancestral Spirits' Realm

The belief in the concept of ghosts follows the belief in ancestral spirits. This is all about spirituality and metaphysics in the minds and lives of the indigenous people. This is when the living people believe that all the

---

[55] Dodo O. (2015) Traditional Taboos Defined: Conflict Prevention Myths and Realities. IDA, Harare.

dead become an invaluable constituency especially to the living; serving as guides, protectors and advisors. It is believed that the dead immediately assume a different form, which is more powerful, mysterious and magical. This belief is not only strong in the Shona people, early philosophers: Plato, Pythagoras and Aristotle have also written widely on the nature of life after death including the roles and powers of the dead[56]. Similarly, Albert Raboteau[57] in *'Slave Religion: The Invisible Institution in the Antebellum South'* and Puckett[58] present how the early slave lives and cultural beliefs were modeled paying particular attention to the world of the dead and their mystical powers. These clearly present how the beliefs in ghosts, powers of the dead and the outer world protected the living and modeled the slaves' lives and cultures.

The elderly strongly believed that the spirit realm could see what the living had no capacity to see; beyond the scope and vision of the living and possibly plan ahead. They also believed that the dead could communicate on their own and possibly craft a solution to a problem affecting the living. This was evident in the belief that if *A* wronged *B*, the ancestors of B could liaise with the ancestors of *A* and agree on an appropriate punishment before *A* was allowed to compensate *A* through

---

[56] Iteyo Crispinous. (2009) Belief in the Spirits of the Dead in Africa: A Philosophical Interpretation. *Journal of the Philosophical Association of Kenya,* Vol. 1/1 p. 147-159

[57] Raboteau, Albert. (1978) Slave Religion the Invisible Institution. Oxford: Oxford University Press.

[58] Puckett, Newbell Niles (2003). Folk Beliefs of the Southern Negro. New York: Kessinger Publishing.

the ancestral spirits. Some of the earthly signs could be seen through the appearance of such spirit world creatures; ghosts (*Chipoko, nyin'inya and tsandukwa*). These are different forms of ghost-like creatures that appear to send a message, to punish an offender of to persecute the living. Their appearance may be at the instigation of either the dead or the living people but through the use of magical powers.

Chieftainship/Kingship

Early Zimbabwean societies recognized the institution of Chieftainship/Kingship as the top most and most powerful in political, social, religious and economic governance. In this discussion, we give prominence to chieftainship because it was and is still the common position in traditional leadership. The chief represented the supernatural on earth, the chief judge, the military supremacy and was the link between the sacred world and the physical cosmos. The type of chieftainship in Zimbabwean societies was that of an earthly being in the costume of holiness, which endowed on the individual, the power to issue out authority that cannot be questioned.

The chiefs had the ultimate authority to maintain law and peace besides being also responsible for the availability of direction, speed, values, opportunity and process in conflict resolution[59]. Chiefs were considered dynamic negotiators, mediators and judges whose legality on the throne, the investiture of kingly authority, their ceremonial cleansing capability, their understanding of the past towards grasping the customs and guidelines bestowed on them by their ancestors, the esteem and

[59] Lemarchand, R. (1977). African Kingships in Perspective – Political Change and Modernization Settings Great Britain: Frank Cass & Co. Ltd.

veneration conferred on them by their followers were prerogatives of contributing immeasurably to peace process and development in their local communities. The chiefs were the overseers for the morality and proprietary of behaviors for both the young and the elderly in societies. Actually, the foundation of unity and mutuality was good morality and action designed for social development in local communities[60].

Ancestors

Ancestors and ancestresses are the long dead who are believed to be still living in some space which is equivalent to the biblical heaven. Ancestors and ancestresses are a respected and feared constituency so much so that whatever is commanded in the name of the dead is complied with. It is believed that they are able to see and direct earthly activities from wherever they are and that they have the ability to communicate with ancestors of other families, communities and ethnic groups regardless of language and cultural differences. Ancestors are believed to be responsible for the living's capabilities, successes and challenges and the interpretations differ with ethnic and cultural backgrounds. It is therefore according to the traditional beliefs, their supernatural capabilities that they are able to resolve conflicts amicably and sustainably.

The relationship between the living and ancestors exists through spirit mediums who are able to connect the two's communication systems. Ancestors are also believed to be responsible for the general governance of the people. Within the Shona people, it is strongly believed that it is

[60] Ayittey, G.B.N. (1991). Indigenous African Institutions New York: Transnational Publishers, Inc.

the disregard of the ancestors that generates conflicts and misfortunes in the clan and society. Some scholars like C.J. Calhoun argue that the power of the ancestors is omnipresent and unconditional whereas that of the living is limited and contestable[61]. It is therefore because of the power in the ancestors that the living are able to regulate society and that the former wield the authority to ensure successes in conflict resolution. In other words, the ancestors have to bless conflict resolution initiatives if they are to be successful. Besides, they are overseers of good morals, good behaviour, anchors of harmony and peace, and creators of the wisdom of conflict resolution.

Age-Class Stratification

In African traditional social stratification, there is strict consideration of the age, status and sex to determine relevance, identity and development. Age-class stratification also known as age-group or generation class determines the types of friends that one can choose and the circles that one also fits to interact with. Traditionally, appropriate age-class stratification was a pointer for peace and collectivity indicating growth for it is within the right group that one is able to show his/her capabilities[62]. In Shona culture, there is a strong recognition for the social structure and hierarchy where there is a grandfather (*sekuru*), father (*baba*), eldest son (*nevanji*), nephew (*dunzvi*), and aunt (*tete*). Any formal communication,

---

[61] Fortes, M. (1965). "Some Reflection on Ancestor Worship in Africa", *African system of Thought* (eds.) M. Fortes and G. Disesten London: Oxford University Press.

[62] Eisenstadt, S.N. (1954). African Age-groups. A Comparative Study, *Africa,* 14 (1).

decision-making and consultation are supposed to follow that hierarchical structure.

Diplomacy

Traditionally, diplomacy has always been a mechanism for the resolution of conflicts through its value for neighbourhood relations and common understanding. Traditionally, diplomacy as an art of convincing the others was applied in various situations like marriage, funeral rites, and selection of leadership and restoration of order in society amongst others. It was applied through the exchange of envoys, figurative communication tactics, offering gifts, round-table dialogue and extension of invites to dignified rituals and sanctions amongst others. Diplomacy amongst others served to ensure statehood and community development, build pleasant relationship within communities and nurtured harmony in diversity encouraging the spirit of social engineering based on *esprit de corps*. To achieve the above, the process employed the following; development of interest, application of reasonable influence, best exploitation of confidence and a declaration of an ultimatum and the use of figurative messages[63].

Diplomacy in the early societies in Zimbabwe also made use of envoys or emissaries. These were facilitators of development who also further strengthened friendly understanding and links amongst communities. Envoys with strong bravado, creativity and wisdom were either send or exchanged between states or communities primarily to create a relationship and where necessary to speak on behalf of the sending king

[63] Smith, R.S (1989). Warfare and Diplomacy in Pre-colonial West Africa Second Edition, London: James Currey.

or chief[64]. In the Zimbabwean context, the envoy concept was other than representation of the sending state, meant to spy on the host state or chief. To some extent, the intelligence would be used in the formulation of strategy in the event of a conflict or other trade talks.

Hospitality

There are some social norms in the Shona and other Bantu cultures which are meant to build peace, stability and harmony through the creation of conducive environments for negotiations, friendliness and development. These norms are what are termed hospitality and entails depiction of sociable temperament towards others. Hospitality is also taken as a sociological philosophy defining peace and oneness[65]. This may not only be between hosts and guests but also amongst individual strangers living in a community. The three-way axis attendant on hospitality namely host-host mutuality, host-guest cordiality and guest-guest understanding apply in conflict resolution.

Hospitality according to indigenous belief systems is necessitated through the employment of some of these traits; friendly temperament, cultural qualities, humility, goodness of character, and neighbourly community[66]. Once these conditions are created, it becomes easy to foster peace and development in society.

---

[64] Ingham, K (ed.) (1974). The foreign Relations of African States, London.

[65] Argyle, W.J. (1968). The Concept of African Collectivism, *Mawazo,* 1(4.)

[66] Ibid

Governance in Conflict Resolution

Endogenous conflict resolution practices as they were crafted by the earliest conflict resolution practitioners have gradually transformed assimilating more of the exogenous mechanisms thus diluting their relevance and effectiveness. This neutralization of the practices should be seen in light of the fast changing concept around governance systems that traditionally regulated both leaders' conduct and the usage of material resources amongst others. It is the absence of such sound governance practices that conflicts erupted in various communities. Governance has traditionally been reliant on three essential factors; development, ideological alignment and security.

The practice of governance in any society is basically connected to the solidity and oneness of that society. Governance is taken as a political organization in which a genuine government consented to by the people is given power and authority to rule. This is achievable through the government's capability to make order, organisation and administration of the society centered on the rule of law. Such an appropriate and genuine government, as an authority, is mandated to authoritatively assign standards by outlining who gets what, when and how. Whatever governance system would have been chosen is expected to satisfy all the players so that peace and order are maintained. In the pre-colonial Zimbabwe, societies existed because there were people who put it together to achieve development and security founded on the philosophical underpinnings which they designed for themselves; suiting their societal needs and expectations.

The pre-colonial Zimbabwean type of governance was traditionally characterised by various types of conflict resolution and mitigation institutions as discussed under Early Systems. Suffice to highlight that generally, all these systems sought to address the following four classes of conflicts; property ownership, personal integrity, territorial expansion and power and relations with the gods. Such systems were common in almost every community such as; the Zezuru, Karanga, Korekore, Manyika, Ndau, Tavara, Budya, Maungwe and Ndebele. In almost all the local chiefdoms, the powerful chiefs had a Council of subordinates known as *Dare Ramambo* which could then delegate its authority to members of the ruling descent, given the size of the chiefdoms. This was an equivalency of the present day decentralization system of governance. Closely akin to this governance practice was the religious aspect of divination which was considered very important in the practice of conflict prevention and resolution and governance.

The pre-colonial indigenous society showed some moral of good governance. This is evidenced by the manifestation of more unjustified wars and conflicts in the contemporary world than they were in the olden days. This was because the system of governance in the pre-colonial age had all that was essential for good governance and conflict prevention and resolution. If there was a clash between two communities or individuals, the traditional leaders would meet with the elders of the two communities and the religious priests and amicably and sustainably resolve the dispute. Regrettably, these endogenous mechanisms have progressively been wind-swept by foreign infiltration, the nature of the post-colonial state and the developing element of globalization.

Early Systems

Africa in general and Zimbabwe in particular has survived for thousands of years employing various culturally acceptable and community embedded endogenous conflict resolution systems. Each of the various communities and ethnics in Africa has its peculiar approach which produces sustainable resolutions. It is also believed that the sustainability hinges on the spiritual component that is attached[67]. Some of the noted approaches include the following randomly selected; *Abunzi* in Rwanda, *Afikpo* in South-East Nigeria, *Curandeiros* of Mozambique, *Akiriket* in Uganda or *bo-ralekgotla* in Botswana, *Ekika* by the Baganda in Uganda[68], *Guurti* and *Dia* system in Somalia there is also *Micu*, Oromo, Luba *Baasa*, and *Harma Hodhaa* by the *Gumuz* and *Shinasha* of Sudan, *Jir* system of the Tiv in Nigeria, and *Judiyya* in Darfur. Others are *Moots* by the Kpelle of Liberia, *Mable* by the Afar in Ethiopia, *Mokgwa Le Molao* by the Tswana of Botswana and, n*dendeuli* system of Tanzania, *Michu* of Western Ethiopia and *Borana-Oromo-Gadda* system of Ethiopia and *Muma* and *Mummat* by the Pokot of Kenya[69].

As we look at the history of conflict resolution in Zimbabwe from the pre-colonial era, it may be prudent that we also focus on some of the practices that were prominent so that we get a glimpse of how the

[67] Bujo B. (1998) The Ethical Dimension of Community-The African Model and the Dialogue Between North and South, Paulines Publications Africa.

[68] Chapman C. and A. Kagaha, (2009) Resolving Disputes Using Traditional Mechanisms in the Karamoja and Teso Regions of Uganda, Minority Rights International.

[69] Pkalya R, M. Adan & I. Masinde, (2004) Indigenous Democracy: Traditional Conflict Reconciliation Mechanisms Among the Pokot, Turkana, Samburu and the Marakwet (ed.) B. Rabar & M. Kirimi, Intermediate Technology Development Group-Eastern Africa.

conflicts were addressed and possibly compare with the other communities elsewhere. Some of the selected practices include; *dare* (court system), *kunyarara* (silence), *jakwara* (communal task ceremonies), and *bira* (ancestral dance ceremonies), *kuripa* (compensation), *kurova guva* (appeasement of the dead), *kurwa* (fighting), *kutsiva* (retaliation), *ndari* (traditional brews), *ngano* (story-telling), *nhaurirano* (negotiation), and *pfonda* (dance ceremonies), *roora* (marriage), *rufu* (death), and *zviera* (taboo). Others were; *kutengeserana* (economic cooperation), *chipari chematunhu akasiyana* (extended matrimonial alliances), *chipari* (polygyny), inter-clan marriage (exogamy), *kupika* (oath-taking) and *mitambo* (competitions), and *kupira* (sacrifices). There were also *kutama* (migration/withdrawal), *kuzvidzwa* (ostracization), *mhiko dzinoera* (religious rites), *rudo* (love), *ruregerero* (forgiveness) and *kubvumirana pachimwe* (collective approach in decision making) amongst others.

Traditionally, community leaders have been part of the governance system; ruling some aspects and communities in their own rights. Especially the Chiefs, they have been an important cog in the governance system as they were part of the king's judiciary and legislative assembly. Traditional leadership is a wide area which encompasses amongst others the following people; kings, chiefs, headmen, kraal-heads, village-heads, household heads, fathers, eldest sons, eldest daughters and eldest nephews, closest family friends, uncles, aunts and the grand-father. Each of these individuals plays a distinct role in the leadership of the community depending on the seriousness, gravity and urgency of the matter.

Since time immemorial, these leaders have been commanding tremendous power and authority in their respective communities until when the early raids by the Ndebele people were experienced around the early 1800. When the Ndebele people first got into the now Zimbabwe, they raided the indigenous people robbing them of their wealth; cattle and women amongst others. During the process, they forced the local people to surrender their authority and autonomy to the Ndebele and also pay tribute in the form of other valuables like minerals, beasts and artifacts. To a great extent, the coming of the Ndebele and the subsequent intrusion washed away some of the values and adherence to the practices and respect accorded to each of the members of the leadership.

During the early 1840s, the first groups of potential colonialists entered into the now Zimbabwe and conquered the two groups; the Shona and the Ndebele subsequently subjecting them under their authority and rule. To ensure that their plan was effective, they focused towards the erosion of the traditional leadership role and powers. This was to some extent achieved by replacing the original and defiant leaders with allegiant and loyal ones. In some cases, those who would have been removed were executed as a way of sending fear to other would-be transgressors and defiant leaders. Gradually, traditional leaders were left redundant; only playing a suppressing role for the colonialist Europeans.

However, it has to be realized that though the traditional leaders' powers had been compromised, they still had some authority over their subjects especially to resolve conflicts. This power had been reserved to allow them to ensure that the colonialist administrators did not have to attend to the indigenous people's grievances. Besides, they were also expected to contain social uprisings within their communities by attending to some of these conflicts and challenges.

Upon the attainment of Zimbabwe's political independence in 1980, the new regime enacted the Chiefs and Headmen Act and the Community Courts Act[70] as a way of resuscitating some of the powers that had been removed from the traditional leaders by the colonial regime. While the former Act sought to empower the Chiefs and Headmen with the legal authority to administer both human and natural resources within their areas of jurisdiction, the latter sought to empower the same leaders to try cases and resolve conflicts within their areas of jurisdiction. This was another clear way by the new regime towards ensuring that the traditional leaders were able to revive their endogenous conflict resolution mechanisms albeit mixing with the exogenous ones. Further to the above efforts, in 1990 and 1998 the state enacted the Customary and Local Courts Act (No.2 of 1990) and the Traditional Leaders Act[71] (Chapter 29:17) and which also revived some of the Chiefs' lost powers.

At this juncture I wish to point out that the leaders that had been for a long time referred to as traditional leaders had now ceased to be; rather, they were now customary leaders. In my previous publication[72], I defined a traditional leader as one who is customarily and culturally appointed to lead the subjects along the traditional practices. With the contemporary

---

[70] The Government of Zimbabwe (1982). Chiefs and Headmen Act (Chapter 29: 01). Harare. Government Printers

[71] The Government of Zimbabwe (1998).Traditional Leadership Act (Chapter 21:05). Harare, Government Printers.

[72] Dodo O. (2013) Traditional Leadership Systems and Gender Recognition: Zimbabwe. *Journal of Gender and Women's Studies,* Vol. 1/1, p. 29-44.

leadership, they no longer follow any of the cultural practices. Like it is rightly noted by Keulder[73], the once traditional leaders are now defined by modernity, are now educated, have since abandoned their traditional religions for Christianity and now speak in foreign languages. What I have also observed with regards to the influence of Christianity on the local traditions is that when the Europeans came to Zimbabwe, in-order for them to be easily absorbed and accepted by the local people, they accepted to adopt indigenous names. Cases in point include H. M. Pollard who adopted *Kunyaira*, Native Commissioner Campbell who took up *Kamuswera,* Native Commissioner for Chilimhanzi Mansel Edye Weale who adopted *Chinyama* in 1895 and Manuel Antonio de Sousa who also adopted *Guveya* as their local names. When the same European traders and missionaries started to spread their Christian religion, they convinced the indigenous people to adopt Christian names for them to easily appreciate the message and be able to read the bible. In the process, that was to be baptism into Christianity. What is evident in this case is a high degree of tolerance and hospitality on the part of the indigenous people who easily took in strangers into their ranks and structures.

The institution of elders was traditionally one body that was renowned for effective and efficient conflict resolution in the traditional societies in Zimbabwe. It was generally divided into two formations; a single member approach and a Council approach. The former involved a single community elder attending to a conflict and successfully coming up with

[73] Keulder, C. 1997a. "Traditional Leaders and Comparative Experiences in Namibia, Botswana and Zimbabwe", in De Villiers, B (Ed.). *The rights of Indigenous People: A Quest for Coexistence.* Pretoria: Human Sciences Research Council.

a sustainable resolution while the latter saw more than one elder teaming up to help discuss a conflict and drawing a conclusion. What was however interesting with these systems was that their establishments followed a systematic process. Either in the village or community, the general populace would look at the characteristics of the elders; women or men and identify leadership traits like wisdom, maturity, composure, tolerance and the ability to listen and talk effectively, ownership of some wealth and having a successful family. It was some of these virtues that qualified one as an elder capable of handling conflicts.

One who did not own any wealth nor had a stable family was not respected and therefore could not give advice in times of conflicts. The amount of respect that an elder commanded depended on the successes of the previous consultations and to some extent, the stability of his/her family other than the size of that family. Though generally most societies in Zimbabwe were patriarchal in nature, when it came to the elder concept, even women were considered depending on the matters and the gravity of the issues. However, most women elders focused on female related conflicts like marriages. This is not to say that women were shut out from leadership positions and decision making processes.

The '*Vashambadzi*' concept was put in place during the early 1700 in the Rozvi state as a way of facilitating trade with the Portuguese traders who had previously been chased away during the 1670s. The '*Vashambadzi*' concept is equivalent to marketing in the modern world. Primarily, the concept was put in place to coordinate international trade keep some distance between the Rozvi people and the Portuguese traders as a way of maintaining peace and ensuring that the latter did not interfere with the governance system in the state. In other words, it ensured independence of the Rozvi state and promoted creativity and a spirit of entrepreneurship with the people so much so that there was a boom in business especially in the following areas; cattle, goats and sheep rearing, crop farming, pottery, blacksmithing, weaving and basketry manufacturing, specialized iron industry producing tools and weapons, and gold mining and game hunting. Distance had to be maintained between the two groups; Africans and foreigners as the latter also sought to convert the locals religiously. The *Vashambadzi* concept also sought to attend to grievances and conflicts associated with trade, communication, routes and boundaries amongst others.

Trade in the pre-colonial Zimbabwe was an important component of the economy. While the states were largely agricultural in nature, some other activities complimented seasonally. Before the coming of the Europeans, trade was conducted between the indigenous communities especially in commodities like salt, farming implements and jewellery in areas like the Middle Save Valley and the Mapfungautsi Plateau. It to a large extent sustained cordial relationships. After the coming of the Europeans, trade continued and was strengthened and diversified to cover some commodities that were needed by the Europeans. External trade improved the lives of the indigenous communities as it brought with it civilization and modern goods technologically like guns, glasses and refined alcoholic beverages amongst others. External trade also refined indigenous trading systems through the transformation of barter trade to the use of currency which was both user-friendly and easy to carry. This form of trade greatly improved the states' economy so much so that hoe-cultivation, small scale industries such as gold mining, weaving, earthenware and making of ironware were set-up and were able to sustain the surrounding people luxuriously[74] thus addressing resource scarcity and deprivation challenges.

The early people of Zimbabwe were peculiar in the way that they lived and organized their affairs. They followed a communal type of settlement where along ethnic or village lines, they built their economies and cultures. To a large extend, this also helped them address some of the potential conflicts within their settlements and also with other neighbours. Collectively, they could ward off enemies and aggression. Again, collectively they could talk over grievances and conflicts. However, this form of settlement and collectivity was short-lived following the invasion of their settlements by the European settlers who subsequently took over some of the fertile and habitable land.

In 1893, the European settlers occupied some of the best land for both habitation and agriculture pushing the indigenous Africans to poor soils in what officially became known as the Reserves after the enactment of the Reserves Act in 1903. This plot to disarm the indigenous Africans of their land was cemented through the establishment of more laws like the Municipal Act of 1897 which described the settlement conditions for Africans and Boards like the 1903 Rhodesia Native Labour Bureau which helped the Chamber of Mines to force Africans to work in the available mines. The other of such laws was the Land Apportionment Act of 1930 which entrenched the racial partitioning of land in Zimbabwe. The Act partitioned the country into the Reserves which were specifically for indigenous Africans; Alienated Land, which was for Europeans but with limited access to Africans who only visited as workers; and Native Purchase Areas, small scale farms that were created

---

[74] Gann L. H (1965) A History of Southern Rhodesia, London.

for competent indigenous Africans. The 1930 Law was further supported by the Land Apportionment Amendment Act of 1941 and the Land Settlement Act of 1944[75] which again saw the forced mass relocations of Africans from their original homes to semi-arid regions where agriculture was a non-event.

After the Europeans had settled down, there was a deliberate attempt at consolidating their powers through containing the indigenous population. This was achieved through the enactment and establishment of such laws and regulations amongst others as the following: the Native Pass Ordinance of 1902; Immorality Suppression Ordinance of 1903; Southern Rhodesia Native Regulations of 1910; the Masters and Servants Act; Native Affairs Act of 1927; Land Apportionment Act of 1930; Maize Control Act of 1931 and 1934; Cattle Levy Act, 1931 and 1934; and the Reserve Pool Act; the Land Apportionment Amendment Act of 1941; the Land Settlement Act of 1944, the Native Land Husbandry Act (NLHA) of 1951, the Tribal Trust Land Act of 1967 which replaced the NLHA of 1951 and the Tribal Courts Act (TCA) of 1969 amongst others. In response to these laws, there were isolated individuals who took it upon themselves to fight the system which was seen as derogatory, discriminative, unfair and retrogressive.

Two such personalities who challenged the alleged unfairness within the Christian church which was discriminatory in promoting black leaders according to Dodo[76] were Shonhiwa Masedza of Gandanzara in Rusape and Muchabaiwa Momberume of Mafararikwa in Marange who founded

[75] Moyana H. V. (1984) The Political Economy of Land in Zimbabwe, Mambo Press, Gweru.

[76] Dodo O. (2016) Apostolicism and Conflict Resolution: Controversies and Complexities. (Forthcoming)

Johane Masowe Chishanu and Johane Marange respectively. The two churches were a response to a harsh political, social and religious environment which had brought in various conflicts. In other words, they were meant to address a looming conflict in the short term while in the long term, the institutions would also on a daily basis resolve other social, political, and economic challenges in society. What however needs to be clarified is that the two individuals were some of the first boys to be lured into the early western schools that produced the first Manyika academics from around 1909 and therefore might have been influenced by the acquired knowledge then. There were also other individuals and civil and labour groups that fought the system down as a way of resolving grievances in society.

During the Rhodesian era, following the advent of industrialization and the employment of more Africans as labourers, various other conflicts were recorded such as contractual disputes, alleged exploitation, racism and several other unfair labour practices. To address the noted conflicts, there came various Unions and Associations which were also responding to the Masters and Servants Act of 1908, the Pass Laws, and the Native Affairs Act of 1927 amongst others. The most prominent of the early conflict resolution practitioners were Jasper Savanhu who led the Federation of Bulawayo African Workers, Benjamin Burombo with his African Workers' Voice Association and Charles Mzingeli who led Industrial and Commercial Workers' Union. Other prominent indigenous figures were; Reverend Thompson Samkange who led African National Congress (ANC) and his son who then took over, Stanlake Samkange, George Nyandoro, James Chikerema, Edson Sithole and Duduza Chisiza who amongst other laws and policies wrestled the Municipal Act of 1897, the Industrial Conciliation Act of 1934 and the Native Land

Husbandry Act (NLHA) of 1951. By the time that NLHA was suspended in 1962 due to serious opposition by civil organisations and labour bodies, it had managed to impact on about 42% of the Reserves. While there are no names for women who participated in some of these initiatives, it is on record that some did participate especially in the Salisbury Bus Boycott which was organized in August 1956 in protest against bus fare increases by the United Transport Company. While from a layperson's view it appears as if the workers' bodies were to instigate protests and demands for fair labour standards, they also served to resolve both economic and labour conflicts. Actually, the labour bodies served as an effective conflict resolution entity on the ground through deterrence and swift reaction to any reported cases. These movements marked the genesis of fully-fledged formal politics in Zimbabwe.

The coming of the Europeans into Zimbabwe saw a confirmation of the discriminatory settlement amongst the ethnic groups; where each ethnic group was expected to live on its own and further protect its territory and its resources from the other groups. To some extent, in the eyes of the indigenous people, this move was designed to ensure that each group's cultural values are protected and nurtured while to the Europeans, it was a deliberate attempt to create a buffer between different groups so that they did not mobilise around a common cause and that they vacated their good soils. In a well calculated move, people were categorised according to their race, colour and in some cases religious orientation before they were allocated homes; where they eventually found themselves clustered along ethnic or racial lines. Some of the communal areas that were created along ethnic lines include those listed in the table below.

Fig. 2.2 Rural Colonial Settlements

AREA	INHABITANTS
Musengezi	Suthu and Ndebele (Former missionaries from South Africa)
Sabi (Charter)	Zezuru people
Guruve	Korekore people
Gwai	Ndebele people
Gwebu (Buhera)	Ndebele (Former aides of the early European missionaries to Manica)
Mushumbi	Karanga and Maungwe (former political outcasts in their original areas)

The same types of settlements were also seen in all the urban areas where the European planners had allocated 45%[77] of the main urban areas like Harare and Bulawayo to the indigenous peoples' settlements. In cases where people were expected to meet, it was also realized that most groupings were structured following ethnic lines. The European designed settlements meant that a particular ethnic grouping would only encounter specific grievances and in-turn mobilise amongst themselves without any influence from the other settlements. This was a deliberate strategy meant to ensure that there was no inter-ethnic communication especially in times of conflicts. Some of the urban settlements that were created along racial/ethnic lines include those below.

Fig. 2.3 Urban Colonial Settlements

[77] Beach D (1999) Zimbabwe: Pre-colonial History, Demographic Disaster and the University, *Zambezia*, XXVI, (i)

AREA	INHABITANTS
Arcadia (Harare)	Coloured
Belvedere (Harare)	Indians
St Martins (Harare)	Coloured
Mufakose (Harare)	Indigenous Zimbabweans
Florida (Mutare)	Coloured

In the long run, political matters were also developed along the same ethnic/racial lines as people were employed largely according to their ethnic groups rather than their key competences. It was realized that most labour grievances and social challenges were also experienced along particular groupings in society. Some of the early political movements in Zimbabwe like the Zimbabwe African national Union (ZANU) under Ndabaningi Sithole and later Hebert Chitepo and Zimbabwe African People's Union (ZAPU) under Joshua Nkomo were ethnically structured; Shona and Ndebele respectively[78]. The split in the political movements to some extent seriously impacted on the strength that united efforts have on communication and conflict resolution. It worked well for the colonial regime that benefitted from the rivalry between ZANU and ZAPU.

The repeated tug-of-war amongst the political leadership in both ZANU; Sithole, Chitepo and subsequently Robert Mugabe and ZAPU; Nkomo, James Chikerema and Jason Ziyapapa Moyo hampered smooth relations and opportunities for effective and efficient conflict resolution within the

---

[78] Mlambo A. S. (2013) Becoming Zimbabwe or Becoming Zimbabwean: Identity, Nationalism and State-building, *Africa Spectrum*, 48/1, p.49-70.

liberation movements. However, there were other instances when coalitions and collective approaches like the Patriotic Fronts and joint teams during the 1977 Geneva and the 1979 Lancaster Conferences did work positively.

Ethnicity though a contested phenomenon to talk about with regards to early systems of conflict resolution, remains important in the same domain. Naturally, identity is a major factor that is used either to build relationships or the create enmity. I say this is a contested area because there are scholars like Sithole[79] who argue that this was a creation of the early colonialist who imported it from the Roman Empire where it was commonly referred to the primitive or barbarians while others like Gulliver[80] simply take it to mean a distinctive grouping defined by common cultural practices. However, what is common in the two schools' positions is that ethnicity builds some common grounding or force. It was therefore that common grounding that shaped a common understanding or a common perception about some system or practice which eventually led to communities either teaming up to fight or to seek peace.

It was also through the same common systems that some communities had to craft some 'traditions' and 'cultures' around the dos and don'ts. This to some extent saw a practice of sending emissaries to seek peace. In most cases, these emissaries were either related or close to the part

---

[79] Sithole, M. (1986): "The Salience of Ethnicity in African Politics: The Case of Zimbabwe", in: *Ethnic Identities and Prejudices: Perspectives from the Third World.* Paranjpe, Anand C. (Ed.). The Netherlands: E.J. Brill.

[80] Gulliver, P. H. (Ed) (1969): Tradition and Transition in East Africa: Studies of the Tribal Element in the Modern Era. London: Oxford University Press.

being courted for peace. This was done in order to win the heart and trust of the other part. Ethnicity also helped to brew hostilities and bloody conflicts which eventually forced creativity amongst people in as far as the design and modeling of more effective and efficient conflict resolution systems was concerned. In other words, conflicts helped communities to research and create new systems of resolving conflicts.

Influence of the Pre-Colonial Leadership Practice to the Present

It has often been asked if colonialism did affect the development of Africa in any way. It has also been questioned if Africa would have been where it is today had the Europeans not come to Africa. But most importantly, it has been asked whether the past Africa has influenced anything in the present Africa. Answers to some of these questions if given objectively are supposed to enlighten us for several years to come. The same answers are also expected to help Zimbabwe understand its approaches to conflict resolution practices; their past, challenges, successes and how they could be nurtured for generations to come. This in short presents the historical development of the indigenous conflict resolution practices in Zimbabwe.

While Europeans did bring a variety of practices and activities including education, it seems some of the education has not really sunk in the minds and practices of some of the leaders and recipients in Africa and Zimbabwe in particular. While there is evidence of improved economic development outcomes as a result of colonialism, on the education front and conflict resolution, very little is evident on the ground. It may be difficult to say that Africa was in the dark before the coming of the Europeans (obviously depending on what one calls dark) and that while

Africa is past the dark era, some have dragged the darkness with them into the light era. It is important that we take a glance at how the past defined events and how the same past has been dragged into the contemporary and now defining the present through some personalities. In the previous chapters, we discussed what may be termed archaic leadership practices. In this section of the chapter, we now see the similarities between the past and the present practices in relationship to the factors that influence leaders' capacity to attend to conflicts in society.

First and foremost, early leaders were divinely appointed thus attracting respect from across the board whereas the contemporary leaders are either voted along patronage basis or imposed on the people. As a result, the latter leaders command no respect subsequently affecting their ability to resolve conflicts. It has also been noted that early leaders were multi-positioned occupying various influential posts like being the king, commander of the army, head of the trial council, and a high priest amongst others. Similarly, the post-colonial leaders in most of the African states and Zimbabwe in particular retained the pre-colonial structure by occupying the Presidency, Commander-in-chief of the defence forces, Chancellor of universities, and the Sherriff, amongst others. Another similarity between the early leaders and the present crop is in the god-like titles such as His Excellence, father, leader, teacher and the wise-men amongst others. Unlike the post-colonial leaders most of whom are in monogamous marriages, the pre-colonial leaders were characterised by polygynous marriages. It was from some of the wives that the kings drew advice and wisdom. It was also through the spouses that appeals and audience with the king could be facilitated. Some of the kings had concubines in each of the regimental towns who also served as spies. The concubines enjoyed a lot of respect in their towns as part of the royal family. However, they also gathered intelligence that amongst others helped secure the office of the king and providing with the much needed counsel.

Closely akin to the above discussion is the kinship concept which most of the early states adopted in their leadership structures. The divine kingship concept amongst other institutions, practices, customs and ideas were held in common by different peoples in areas remote from each other. The notion of 'divineship' in the leader concentrated power on the king thus allowing him to rule without anyone's oversight. This has also been roped in to the present African leadership where the presidents are seen as divinely appointed and to some extent 'worshipped' by followers.

Summary

Before the coming of Europeans, indigenous people had some ways of addressing their conflicts. These were effective and to some extent, sustainable. They were only tainted after the coming of foreign religions and education systems. The chapter looked at some of the early practices by the indigenous communities and juxtaposed with exogenous systems. The chapter however acknowledges the coming of Europeans and all their associated practices to ensure development and civilisation.

CHAPTER THREE

WOMEN IN CONFLICT RESOLUTION

Introduction

Conflict resolution is a contested arena that has no generally agreed approach. Conflicts manifest differently under various circumstances and driven by various personalities and influences; the resolution approaches also differ. Traditionally, this area has been known, at least in the public domain as a men arena; adjudicating cases, bringing conflicting parties together and mediating hostile enemies amongst others while women are engaged in other household chores. The truth however is that women have also played an almost important role as that of men in conflict resolution since time immemorial. Actually, the truth about the ancient societies in Zimbabwe is that there were more women in traditional leadership positions compared to the modern set-up. This chapter therefore focuses on the role of women in conflict resolution through several of its elements; development, culture and leadership.

Background

In our endeavor to understand the role and place of women in the history of conflict resolution in Zimbabwe since the pre-colonial era, it is important that we look at several other variables and situations that have described African societies in general and the Zimbabwean in particular. This will be done through the discussion of gender, leadership and patriarchy amongst others. There has been a generalized view of women in both leadership and conflict resolution areas by several scholars who unfortunately tend to lump all women as if they are born from a single family that follows a defined culture. I want to put it here that the participation of women in conflict resolution and leadership are driven by gender relations where men and women perform important and noticeable roles in upholding confines for their anticipated "gendered" activities. This, women can only achieve through the method of cooperation and domination both in the public and private domain.

I argue that it is not easy to generalize all women in Zimbabwe as 'just women'. There is an influence of 'gender' as it is understood culturally, economically, socially and politically. First and foremost, gender is generally defined as a socially constructed role allocation. What it therefore means is that the Zimbabwean society quietly allocates roles to both men and women based on 'just that' outside of biological features and built. In the Zimbabwean context just like several other cases, gender and conflict resolution are understood as functioning on various overlapping stages; place, time, community, culture, level of literacy and level of civilisation, nature of the task, other parties involved and the nature of relationship and conduct shared amongst others. However, amongst the above cited variables, some are more influential than others. In this instance, there is need for an understanding of the effect of culture on gender socialisation, stereotyping, tasks and the standing of women amongst others. Culture involves the entirety of a society's rules, *raison d'etre*, principles, creed, ethics, philosophy and ideology. It comprises communal knowledge and education and how it is conveyed from one generation to another determining the way social institutions model life. Culture as a generally standardized behaviour and way of life for a particular community has for ages defined how various Zimbabwean constituencies conduct themselves both in public and private. It has also inculcated a sense of hardworking and bravery in some women so much so that they are able to stand any situations and make instantaneous decisions depending on the situation. This ability to stand any heat and make instantaneous and appropriate decisions by women is what makes good leadership. Such qualities in the olden days in Zimbabwe were seen in women possessed by ancestral spirits, traditional healers and some other women socialised in leadership circles. Closely akin to the above is also a need to understand women's particular leadership and conflict resolution experiences in a Zimbabwean context vis-a-viz other African gender perceptions and general world views[81]. The long and short of it is that to a large extend, in Zimbabwe and in the olden days, gender was defined and influenced by most of the cited factors.

Our discussion on gender, leadership and conflict resolution has to be polished for clarity and this clarity also demands a look at the structure of society as it is driven by patriarchy as a governance model. While

[81] Dodo O; G. Dodo & M. Zihanzu (2017), African women in traditional leadership role in Zimbabwe: The Case of Shona, *African Journal of Democracy and Governance*, 4(1&2), 133-158

there is an acknowledgement and serious affirmation on the existence of matriarchy in some sections of the society, the majority are patriarchal. Patriarchy is all over; the ancestral spirit realm structure and in Christianity through the concept of trinity. Over time and influenced by globalisation and civilisation, women are now being exposed to various leadership opportunities that are emerging from numerous interrelated and dynamic contacts functional on diverse levels.

Elliot and Stead[82] add that women leaders derive motivation and support to lead and pursue conflict resolution initiatives in society from role models, relationships, mentors and social networks which are traditionally found and nurtured through permanent systems of leadership and socialisation. Such systems include social hierarchical structures and other social and political functionalities like spirit mediums, Headwomen and kings and chiefs' wives amongst others. These also determined development which is also a facet of conflict resolution. From the pre-colonial era, development has been a responsibility of all members of the society by virtue of their contribution regardless of how small or light it was. In the case of women's role in development, there is a lot of literature and evidence to support the invaluable role played by women since time immemorial. It has been shown in other chapters and areas in this discussion that while men took up the manual work in development, some of the ideas and decisions were made by women through and in various forums. From the Kings right to the newly married couple in society, the wife has been known to wield a lot of influence in decision making; what to construct at home, the crop and hactarage to grow, when to relocate and where,

[82] Elliott, C. and Stead, V. (2009). Women's Leadership. London: Palgrave Macmillan.

who to social with and share beer with and when to bear other children amongst others.

Contrary to some scholars' (Harcourt[83] and Soetan[84]) arguments that women have not been visible in most development debates and circles, I argue that the reality on the ground with regards to the Zimbabwean scenario from a traditional feminist economic view-point is that it has been women either deputizing men or coming up with ideas that unfortunately 'are considered some other time' so that they appear as if they are crafted by men. Besides, unless we fail to agree that reproduction and the creation of human resource, the production of subsistence food and the caring of the young, old and sick are elements of development, then we conclude that indeed women played no important role in development.

Ancient Feminine Approaches

In the ancient times, male leaders were known to rebel at some point of their leadership against their seniors and kings regardless of their relationship to the king. Therefore, the appointment of female leaders (headwomen, chiefs and governors) was a counter measure to the royal sons and other male leaders and maintained a centralized power structure in the kingdom. Some of the women leaders' roles included; advising the

[83] Harcourt W. (1994). Feminist Perspectives on Sustainable Development, London: Zed Books.

[84] Soetan R. O. (2001) Culture Gender and Development. A Report submitted to the African Institute for Economic Development and Planning (IDEP), Dakar, Senegal, October 2001. The Centre for Gender and Social Policy Studies, Obafemi Awolowo University, Ile-Ife, Nigeria.

king, settle disputes and share deceased property. Of all the recorded kingdoms[85], the Manyika and Teve which was to the South-east of Manyika had more female leaders than any other. In these kingdoms, women were appointed to lead from the ward level and were called '*vazvari*'. However in the Manyika kingdom, women played an unusually important role of helping the king's governance through a female ancestral spirit called Nyamandoto. The spirit manifested through the king's sister called '*semukadzi*'.

Presently in independent Zimbabwe, there have only been a total of 5 female traditional leaders whereas during the pre-colonial era, there were over ten in the few states that were there. The Hwata chiefdom had a female chief from 1820 to 1837. The second Hwata chief was Minge, an elder daughter of Shayachimwe Muombami who acted on behalf of her younger brother called Kamuteku. She however surrendered power to her half-brother called Kaviya Zaranyika after she failed to deliver. Like I indicated earlier on that there were more female leaders within the Manyika kingdom, King Tendai assumed power in 1874-5 and immediately according to Bhila, effected three prominent changes. The first of the changes was that he forbade his daughters to marry and arranged concorts for his daughters and sisters taking all the children born out such illegitimate relationships to be his. He also created wards for his daughters and sisters to run and ensured that no in-law got involved as a way of securing his authority and leadership. Following these changes, Tendai appointed the following females as headwomen; Kanganya in north-west Manyika, Sherukuru in Manyika, Manunure,

---

[85] Bhila H. H. K. (1982) Studies in Zimbabwean History: Trade and Politics in the Shona Kingdom. The Manyika and their Portuguese and African Neighbours, 1575-1902, Longman, UK.

Wisa in Nyamukwarara Valley, Mpotedzi in Honde Valley, Risineuta in Zengeni area near Penhalonga, Nyakuwanikwa in Penhalonga, Chikanga and Muredzwa. The establishment of the Southern Rhodesia Native regulations of 1898 saw the abolition of the hereditary selection of traditional leaders and replaced with a politicized approach. As a result, in 1934, the following women leaders were deposed by the colonial regime: Mupotedzi of Honde valley, Sherukuru of Manyika and Kanganya also of Manyika. There were several other prominent women in leadership positions of the likes of Shinyamira who led the early phases of the resistance to taxation by Europeans in the early 1890s, Charwe (medium of Mbuya Nehanda[v]) who was executed by the British led court in the central plateau following allegations that she had ordered the killing of Henry M. Pollard Kunyaira by Hwata in Shopo, now Chiweshe in 1896[86]. Apparently, Pollard was an oppressive Native Commissioner for Mazoe who had lost Charwe's carriers which the latter had entrusted him. Beach and other researchers including my own analysis of the original BSC Police diary, call this a private quarrel. However, when Charwe was tried, the impression that was presented and which the present politicians seek to portray is that Charwe was executed for leading the 1896 resistance to the British South African Company activities. After Charwe, in 1906, another medium of Mbuya Nehanda called Mativirira[vi] came into being and led both in governance and conflict resolution.

Women did command an important position in the local governance systems and conflict resolution practices. It is clear that while women in these early societies did not own much in terms of immovable property,

[86] According to an original manuscript diary by the BSA Police of Mazoe Fort (1896) referenced Alderson Papers AL1/1/1.

they had an important decision. They had a say in the migration of a family. If there were shortages of either water or firewood, it was the woman who could push for relocation as she was responsible for the fetching of both water and firewood. The same also applied in the case of food shortages. Whenever a family experienced a drought, it was the women who could push for a search of another piece of land where water for both consumption and agricultural purpose was in abundance. This was because women were responsible for food security in the home. There is however another argument that has been proffered by scholars like Snyder[87] who dispute that while there is this general belief, the wealth in the home was traditionally owned by women. Men were, according to this belief only custodians. This is explained in the argument that if a woman dies, all the movable property is taken away by her relatives and leaves the man with nothing whereas if a man dies, the property is left for the family except in isolated cases where some greedy uncles and aunts grab the property for their own use. Women also played several other roles in governance and conflict resolution. Witch-doctress Nyanda who lived in the Granite Kopje (now Harare) and another unidentified woman intelligence operative of the Hwata group who was captured by the British policemen on her way from Amandas (now Concession) to Salisbury are some of the women who represent the importance of women in conflict resolution. These women were key players in the organisation of resistance and clashes with the European settlers.

Culturally, it is known that wives have the capacity to persuade and convince their husbands on matters of decisions and they do it in their

[87]Snyder M. (2000) Women and African Development: Bibliography Essays. Choice: Current Reviews for Academic Libraries, Vol. 36 (Feb).

bedrooms where they wield more and strategic control. To buttress this argument is Becker[88] who gave out in her research that women in the past had a substantial stake in political power and customary leadership and that they could also discuss power in the sexual and economic lives. While there is an acknowledgement that most African societies including the pre-colonial Zimbabwe were strictly hierarchical and patriarchal in nature as posited by Gaidzanwa[89], Oyewume[90] and Amadiume[91], women still had their space in most families due to their positions either as elderly children or as senior wives (*vahosi*) in a polygynous marriage, simply strategically positioned by virtue of being the eldest wives (*maiguru*) due to their marriage to the eldest son in the family or the king's sister (*tete*) who from a distance played the aunt's role of influencing events. It should be realized that traditionally, though women

[88]Becker H. (2000) A Concise History of Gender, Tradition and the State in Namibia, in Keulder C. (ed) '*State and Democracy: A Reader in Namibian Politics*. Windhoek, Gamsberg MacMillan, p.171-199.

[89]Gaidzanwa R. (1992) Bourgeois Theories of Gender and Feminism and their Shortcomings with Reference to Southern African Countries, in Meena R. (ed) *Gender in Southern Africa: Conceptual and Theoretical Issues*. Harare, SAPES.

[90] Oyewume O. (1997) The Invention of Women: Making African Sense of Gender Discourse. US, University of Minnesota Press.

[91]Amediume I. (2000) Daughters of the Goddess, Daughters of Imperialism: African Women, Culture, Power and Democracy. London, Zed

[92] Davison J. (1997) Gender, Lineage and Ethnicity in Southern Africa, Westview Press, US.

[93] Mudenge S.I.G. (1986). Christian Education at the Mutapa Court, Zimbabwe Publishing House, Harare.

did not sit in the decision-making councils, there were isolated cases where some selected women could be members and even military commanders[92]. Such people could be drawn from the royal family such as the queen mother (mother to the king) and the king's senior wife (*vahosi*). This was the case with the influence of King Negomo Mapunzagutu's mother then known as Dona Maria[vii] (Lady Mary) following her baptism by a Roman Catholic priest Gonzalo da Silveira during a Council meeting that upheld death sentence on Silveira[93]. Though most of the family valuables were legally owned by men in the family, women had their valuables which could not be taken by men without their consent. Such were household valuables, the kitchen hut and sometimes some pieces of land especially those closest to the village. In most matters involving these cited valuables, women's voice was respected.

In the olden days, the traditional courts and conflict resolution systems also had a provision of appeals against set decisions and judgments. The appeals could be made through basically two set routes; through the members of the ruling council and through the royal family members. The former had access to the king and could also bring the issues for discussion informally with the king at various forums. Appeals through the royal family members could be channeled through the queen mother who commanded a lot of respect from both the king and the entire council. Alternatively, some could appeal through the king's senior wife who wielded a lot of influence in private domain. The senior wife could influence the king's decisions behind the scenes in a manner that even an almost passed court verdict could be reversed at the last minute. Though the families were patriarchal in nature, the king's sisters especially the eldest had a special position that she could even challenge the king. It was therefore through that power that some people could appeal through the sisters.

From a cultural and religious view-point, women played an equally important role in both conflict resolution and ritual management practices. There is affirmation that the possession of an individual by an ancestral spirit had nothing to do with one's sex; rather it was about capacity to shoulder the tasks, age, and nature of relationship with the spirit and sometimes the level of belief in the practice. Therefore, there were an almost equal number of female mediums as that of male mediums in ancient Zimbabwe. However, besides the above, women also had an important role of determining the coming of the spirits during ceremonies through singing, ululating, clapping and dancing. These ceremonies were important in that they; brought people together in society, re-connected relationships, appeased spirits, created communication between the dead and the living thus resolving disputes and helped communities understand their future for forward-looking planning purposes amongst others.

Summary

In the traditional African societies, men are at the top of the societal hierarchy. However, women are pivotal in the decision-making processes either as the parties making the decisions or influencing the responsible men in leadership positions. It is this crucial responsibility by women and their ability to steer social, political, religious and economic activities that the chapter did discuss. In this chapter, we looked at the background to women leadership and their influence in daily community development since time immemorial. It was also specifically important to focus on some of the ancient approaches to conflict resolution by women and or processes that involved women. The chapter basically enlightened us on the place of women in traditional conflict resolution in Zimbabwe since the earliest states.

CHAPTER FOUR

EXOGENOUS CONFLICT RESOLUTION

Introduction

It has been proved beyond any reasonable doubt that Africans in general and Zimbabweans in particular had their endogenous systems of resolving conflicts. These systems came in various forms. The coming of the Europeans into Africa had a serious effect and impact on the lives of the indigenous peoples in as far as conflicts and their resolution strategies were concerned. It is these forms of strategies that were imported into Africa commonly called exogenous systems that this chapter seeks to discuss. The discussion looks at the effects of the exogenous conflict resolution systems on the local scene, explore their various forms and roles and to some extent, understand the contribution of the church in these efforts.

Education and Conflict Resolution

Conflicts are caused by a variety of factors that are also influenced by amongst others, resource availability, level of literacy, the demographic structure, type of leadership, shared ideology and the types of subjects in the area. This chapter therefore discusses the role of education in conflict resolution. It looks at the subject from a two-pronged perspective: the first being that the more a society is uneducated the more they are unable to flex their minds to make sound and acceptable decisions. Secondly, the chapter argues that education has often been misconstrued as a yardstick for sustainable development and a guarantee for peace. These two positions are in direct contrast but seek to send an important message which is controversial though.

Why should we study traditional practices in this modern day and age of science and technology? Well, it is imperative to underline the point that whereas societies are ever-changing and changes are unavoidable, the fundamental philosophies and ideals of a people must be enthusiastically safeguarded and passed on from one age group to the other. It is best that history be appraised in light of the contemporary efforts to shape the kind of society people desire. It is important to realize that education in this context is seen from two broad lenses; western education and indigenous education systems. The former is that type of education that involves the dissemination of knowledge from the formally qualified to teach. This type of knowledge mainly involves westernized practices and prepares the recipient for the globalized world where various cultures, practices, beliefs, technologies and lifestyles are the order of the day. This type of education involves reading and writing as the major elements sharpening one's intelligence. The latter type of education is characterised by the dissemination of knowledge from the elderly and experienced to the younger generations through story-telling and practice. This mainly involves the ability to interpret and lead important rituals and to execute important household tasks. In this type of education, the level of literacy is determined by one's depth of wisdom and ability to make instant and wise decisions. Therefore, when a person is considered uneducated from a western perspective, he/she may be the most educated from a Zimbabwe indigenous society point of view. In short, the traditional Zimbabwe's level of education is measured in terms of wisdom inherent in an individual.

The Coming of Western Education

When the first Europeans got into the now Zimbabwe, they had various agendas in mind but chief amongst them were mining ventures and markets for their industrial products. However, to achieve their objectives, the Europeans had to use religion as their bait to weaken the indigenous peoples' resolve for sovereignty. They also had to colonize the land so they could enjoy all the authority to control and exploit the resources; human and natural.

In order for the Europeans to communicate effectively with the local people, they first and foremost had to learn the local languages and in the process ended up corrupting some of the dialects and indigenous words. No wonder why there is no more letter '*L*' in all the Shona dialects. Again, some of the locals were taught some of the European languages so they could be used as role models in their communities in their endeavor to mobilise more indigenous volunteers. For the Europeans to be easily acceptable within the African settings, they also adopted local identities as discussed in Chapter Two.

It was later on around the 1890s that the Europeans established their early formal schools around the country in their endeavor to win the hearts and minds of the indigenous people. Precisely it was the Christian missionaries who came up with the idea of formal education outside of government efforts for the indigenous communities before they built learning centres in a manner that attracted more potential learners[94]. To

---

[94] Katola M. (2014) Incorporation of Traditional African Cultural Values in the Formal Education System for Development, Peace Building and Good Governance, *European Journal of Research in Social Sciences*, Vol. 2/3, p. 31-39

ensure that more local people got exposed to education and in indigenous languages, most of the missionaries established centres around the territory as follows; the Jesuits' Empandeni of 1896 enrolled 350 pupils whilst in 1901[95] the rest were established as follows; the Anglicans at St Augustine's Penhalonga , the American Methodists at Old Umtali, and the Mariann-hill fathers at Triashill together produced Manyika; the Jesuits at Chishawasha, near Salisbury, produced Zezuru and enrolled 90 pupils; and the Dutch Reformed Church at Morgenster produced Karanga, St Columbus under Church of England in Bulawayo which enrolled 95 pupils and the American Foreign Mission at Mt Selinda, South Melsetter which enrolled 80 pupils. On the other side, the BSAC administration also established schools and one of the earliest of such native institutions is Pednor farm primary school in Bindura which was opened in 1895. Immediately after establishing these centres, they produced and subsequently absorbed some of the early local academics to help spread the education and motivate others. Such individuals were Mark Kanogoiwa, Enoch Sanehwe, David Mandisodza, Joseph Nyamurowa, Paul Mariyanga and Jason Machiwanyika[96]. It was education that perfected some of the endogenous conflict resolution systems.

When the Europeans established schools, they were categorised into the following three; Class 1 school had 180 days holiday per year, had boarding facilities and was under European supervision; Class 2 school has 2 hours of schooling daily for 180 days a year, instruction was in

[95] McIlwaine (1901) Report of the Inspector of Schools Upon Education Presented to the Legislative Council: 31/03/1901 by Acting Inspector R. McIlwaine.

[96] See Beach

English but not industrial subject, was a day school and under European supervision and Class 3 school was run by native teachers and taught to speak and understand English[97]. Over time, this approach to education was revisited by Jowitt, the Director of Native Development when in 1929 he transformed the education system so that it could address the needs of the learner through the growth of socially desirable knowledge, attitudes and skills. Jowitt elaborated on what his predecessor Keigwin had attempted to put into practice at Domboshava and Tsholotsho schools of industrial training in the early 1900s. Domboshava was a skills training school for men while Tsholotsho was for women.

Since the establishment of formal schools in Zimbabwe, by 1919 and 1927, according to a Report of the Director of Education L. M. Foggin, 1900 to 1920 and the Department of Education Returns of 1927, there were 39381 and 97051 pupils in all the three classes of schools and a total of 696 and 1478 schools respectively as defined by Foggin. All the schools then were primary schools. The distribution of the statistics is as follows as at 1927[98].

Fig 4.1 Enrolment Statistics

		1919		1927
	SCHOOL	ENROLMENT	SCHOOL	ENROLMENT
1ST CLASS	24	1692	60	4160
2ND CLASS	39	3696	67	6470
3RD CLASS	607	32491	1351	86421
EVENING	26	1502		
TOTAL	696	39381	1478	97051

[97] Education Department Returns: Abstracts from Department of Education Reports, 1908-1917 and 1927, South Rhodesia (original script).

[98] Report of the Director of Education, 1900 to 1920 (original script).

To ensure smooth and consistent continuity in the development of schools, various teachers training institutions were established so much so that by 1929, there were 1723 African teachers in primary schools and that in 1934 alone, 100 trained teachers passed out of the various training institutions[99]. To develop the quality of students who were being produced in the available schools, Father Alban Winter, the Principal of St Augustine's Penhalonga (1935-39) went a step further by introducing the first secondary school with 6 students in 1939. Other secondary schools were later established including Goromonzi School in 1946 with 202 boys and 31 girls.

Roles

While education the world over is meant to serve various but developmental roles, it has been abused and its efforts directed towards irrelevant objectives. It should be realized that the objectives of education in the olden days differs vastly from what is expected nowadays. However, at the end of the day, what is important is to establish the planned goals and what really comes out. According to Sir James Graham who chaired the Committee of Enquiry into Native Affairs in 1911, the development of African education rested almost entirely in the hands of missionary authorities who amongst others; taught peace and tolerance, taught them to read and understand skills,

[99] Department of Native Education Report of 1934, p.7.

[100] Atkinson N. D. (1974) A History of Educational Policy in Southern Rhodesia. PhD Thesis to University of London.

availed industry-focused knowledge[100] and taught them to read the bible. Broadly however, education plays the following roles; preventative, protective, and transformative. However, there are other specific roles that education facilitates on the ground and these change from one area to another and also based on several other variables. Whether in the ancient times or nowadays, knowledge helps a society to appreciate their being and all the values that they treasure. This at the end of the day defines a people and their sovereignty as they are able to protect their heritage from external intrusion and dilution. Some societies believe that failing to protect their cultures and beliefs is a sign of lack of knowledge and the most relevant education. Education is supposed to safeguard what is relevant and important to a people.

It has been realized that both cultures and societies are highly dynamic as they mutate always. This mutation allows other elements to fall away others joining in while others are completely disfigured. Often times, societies that change in structure and ideology allow impurities to tarnish their outlook hence the need for preventative education which stops the mutation process from washing away the originality of a people and their cultures. The third role of education as cited above is to transform a society. Either a society is transformed to allow vast changes which ultimately neutralize the value in that group of people or that a society is transformed into a group of thick-headed people who take no exogenous influences regardless of the outcome.

---

[101] Aragon, J. and Vegas, M. (2009) Governance Evidence In Peru: Production and Use in the Education Sector, UNDP, Oslo Governance Centre, Discussion Paper 19.

Governance according to Aragon and Vegas[101], especially in the area of policy making is improved. Most people who acquire knowledge especially formal tend to experience a changed environment. It has been noted that the level and nature of argument that is proffered by an educated person differs from one who is not. Similarly, the policies that are crafted by an informed and educated people are different from those designed by an ignorant and illiterate people. The former is defined by logic, reason, and information while the latter focuses on authoritarianism, suppression of people's desires and cruelty amongst others. Closely akin to good policy formulation and its subsequent implementation is the issue about good governance. Good governance is only possible if the policies and laws are allowing having been designed taking cognizance of the various needs of the masses like freedoms, democracy, human rights, constitutionalism and proper and adequate social services' provision.

Education is also important in helping people to appreciate their identities, their formation and the relationships that they share with their neighbours. The level of education in a people helps them understand identity factors. Identity factors are important for understanding conflict as they also expose differences between identity-based groups commonly known as 'horizontal inequalities'. Education has a history of enlightening the masses to be able to see what is beyond what others see like social, political and economic inequalities in society. It also allows people to be flexible especially when it comes to critiquing the surrounding world from a reasoned philosophy. This is what really motivated the first secondary school students' protest at Dadaya Mission School in 1947. The protest though relatively violent, was meant to resolve some long standing grievances by the indigenous people. In essence, the protest was an effective deliberate mechanism for resolving conflicts. Education has also brought people together creating a completely new and solid community of intellectuals. There are instances when strangers are mistaken for close relatives on account of their closeness and friendly relationship. This has been experienced in cases where people migrate in search of education and probably start to relate along ethnic, religious or place of origin lines. Gradually, a distinct community is founded.

Western education has over the years been used for various uses; development and conflict. It has especially in Africa managed to open up communities' mindsets to accept dynamism in different spheres; political, religious, economic, social and cultural. While Africa in general and Zimbabwe in particular have had their form of development that combatted poverty and conflicts, the European types of development were better, flexible and more effective. This has over the years helped in combating poverty through technologisation and industrialization. However, according to Shamuyarira[102], in the 1970s, literacy rate was higher in Africans than it was in Europeans; 40% and 20% respectively. Shamuyarira argues that the Europeans simply wanted to create a pool of literate Africans who would work in their factories. What must be noted is that literacy levels are calculated using the statistics of people who can read and write at basic level. This is explained by the fact that of the 68 614 primary school leavers in 1975, only 7831 proceeded into secondary schools while the other 55 446 graduates were unaccounted. During the same period, the number of Africans in jobs fell by 7 000[viii]. Therefore, ~~Europeans just wanted a labour-~~force that could take instruction, operate

[102] Shamuyarira N. (1978) Education and Social Transformation in Zimbabwe, Development Dialogue (2); Dag Hammarsskjold Centre, Sweden.

machinery, read and possibly submit situational reports. During the colonial era, no Africans were either allowed to join the civil service till 1961 or taken for apprenticeship training until in 1962. This is the same situation in the present Zimbabwe with regards to literacy levels that are reported to be over 92%. Interestingly, out of the reported 92% literate Zimbabweans, only 8% are educated up to tertiary level, the rest are basic educated and therefore not economically productive as they lack scientific and scholarly initiative, creativity, objectivity, imagination and ingenuity

If the Europeans had only brought technology and industries without education, no indigenous people would have been able to operate the machinery or be initiative and creative enough to establish their own industries. It has been shown in various studies that western education brought with it the following; tolerance, wisdom, patience, intelligence, craftsmanship, honesty, prudence, and flexibility amongst its products. It was then within these products that the above cited virtues were broadly disseminated into the majority of the people who lacked them. Closely related to the virtues cited above, education established some sense of tolerance and patience in the people so much so that whenever there were conflicts in society, the educated could then come in and moderate the talks for an amicable position. This to some extent explains the existence of intellectuals in society who then sort of lead the rest of the communities in both dialogues and developmental issues.

The role of the intellectuals is not only seen in the post-colonial Zimbabwe, it was evident in times since immemorial but became pronounced soon after the establishment of the early European schools in the early 1900s. Further, this is seen in the formation of the early labour and political movements in the 1930s going into the 1970s when those who had either attended schools in Zimbabwe or those who had been abroad were able to explain the prevailing situations then and ended up founding some of the civil society institutions.

Western education has played a crucial role in the conflict resolution area. It has been realized that most of the educated people have acquired the knowledge required to stand their ground in the event of an argument. In other words, western education builds confidence in the vulnerable groups. The level of women participation in governance systems was to some extent restricted due to some cultural beliefs and practices. Following the advent of western education, a clearly defined concept of participation and accountability was created. Accountability implies the ability to call community leaders to account for their policies and actions. In this regard, accountability meant that the leaders had to respond to the expectations of their subjects. Similarly, participation is also meant to create an arena for conducive debate on topical and important issues and participate directly or indirectly in day-to-day governance matters including decision-making. It is however not always that participatory decision-making is smooth as it may be challenged. This therefore means that conflict resolution measures have to be in place to manage disagreements.

Education especially in the developing world creates gaps between people particularly of opposite sex. Emanating from a patriarchal governance system that prioritised boys ahead of girls, most women have not had an opportunity of getting education like their fellow men. This has naturally discriminated them from good jobs and social and political advancement. Men have remained superior to women in most instances though there are some changes due to modernity and the adjustments to the gender laws.

Gender roles in most patriarchal societies have to a large extent been defined not only by culture; the level of education attained has also played a pivotal role. Besides, people in general have been allowed to show-case their capabilities through education. Therefore, education has helped expose other peoples' weaknesses leading to conflicts. In other words, there has been serious competition in most communities emanating from the effects of education.

The Church in the Conflict Resolution Architecture

The church was the fore-runner to the colonization of Africa. It was the bible in the hands of some men and women who had been trained to be peaceful, tolerant, patient and soft in their approach that was used to confuse, divert attention and defraud the locals of their freedoms and sovereignty. However, for the church to win the hearts and minds of the local people, they capitalized on poverty, diseases, backwardness and lack of effective weaponry amongst others defining the locals. It was a carrot and stick situation which gradually stole the Africans' liberties and simultaneously brought them to civilisation. It must be understood that the church; Christianity and Islam served the same purpose of bringing civilisation, development and perfecting peace amongst others. The church also through education ensured that people in their civil conditions developed some senses of tolerance, order, literacy, intelligence, wisdom, harmony, patience and reason amongst others as attributes for effective development, peace-building and conflict resolution. Therefore, this discussion looks at the churches' position in the conflict resolution matrix in Zimbabwe over the period.

Missions in Zimbabwe

Following the fall of the two; Shona and Ndebele kingdoms in 1893/4, the development of a capitalist economy led to the development of a Christian society as various religious groups rushed into Zimbabwe to establish missionary stations. In Matebeleland, there were basically seven church societies which effectively established themselves. The London Missionary Society (LMS) was established at Inyati and the resident missionary was Bowen Rees who was a strong believer in ethnic superiority of the Ndebele *Zansi*. It also opened Hope Fountain mission with C. D. Helm who also participated in the Rudd Concession of 1888 manning. In 1895, Cullen Redd opened Dombodema Mission while LMS deployed David Carnegie to open Centenary Mission in 1897[103].

There was also the Jesuit Zambezi Mission (JZM) which was based at Empandeni with Father Peter Prestage and Andrew Hartmann. In 1892, JZM opened a series of stations at the following; Embakwe, 8 miles south-west of Empandeni, Silima, 7 miles north-west, Kitwe, 6 miles north-east and Mkaya, 6 miles to the north of Empandeni Mission. In 1921, it also opened St Joseph Mission in Semokwe district. The Seventh Day Adventist (SDA) opened its mission at Solusi farm in 1895 while the Brethren in Christ opened in Matopo and Insiza areas. The Church of England had various missions in Bulawayo and Wankie (now Hwange) while the Church of Sweden was stationed in Belingwe (now

[103] Bhebe N. (1979) Christianity and Traditional Religions in Western Zimbabwe, 1859-1923, Longman, Britain.

Mberengwa) and Selukwe (now Shurugwi). The Wesleyan Methodist Missionary Society established itself in 1895 in Matebeleland region. Other missions were later established as follows; in 1897, Tegwani Mission under C. M. Temple, Zuzumba station in 1903 under Moses Mfazi and the Selukwe circuit of 1908 which was under H. J. Baker[104].

In Mashonaland region, there were various missionary societies that also established themselves. In Manica were the Church of England at St Augustine's Penhalonga, the American Methodists at Old Umtali (now Mutare), and the Mariann-hill fathers at Triashill in Rusapi (now Rusape); the Jesuits at Chishawasha, near Salisbury (now Harare); the Dutch Reformed Church at Morgenster in Fort Victoria (now Masvingo) and the American Foreign Mission at Mt Selinda, South Melsetter.

What must be realized is that wherever missionaries established their stations, they ensured that all the spirit mediums and their related rituals were demonized before they were condemned. This explains why places like Mt Darwin, Muzarabani, Guruve and Rushinga amongst others still have the spirit medium concept. To a great extent, the agenda of the white missionaries to neutralize and dissolve all the traditional belief systems in Africa in general and Zimbabwe in particular was a success.

Summary

It has been acknowledged in the previous chapters that indigenous societies had valuable and effective conflict resolution systems before the coming of Europeans. However, the acceptance of other ethnic and racial groups into the Shona communities meant some preparedness on

---

[104] See Bhebe

the part of the local people to assimilate them into the social, political and economic systems. It has been pointed out in the chapter that especially the coming of the Europeans brought the much needed education and more tolerant and flexible approaches to conflict resolution. The Europeans also brought a new religion which out-rightly transformed the indigenous peoples' lifestyles; fostering development and eroding cultural values. It was again in this chapter that the roles of education and Christianity in conflict resolution processes were explored.

CHAPTER FIVE

CONFLICT RESOLUTION CHALLENGES

Introduction

Traditionally in Shona societies, conflict resolution was time-focused, time driven and time-specific. Conflict resolution as a method was conducted with reference to the element of time which allowed worthy consideration and maximum concern. Although, it is known time does not respect individuals and issues, it links with activities, seasons and rituals. Like the biblical phraseology; *there is time for everything*. Whenever conflict resolution was conducted, the stakeholders would firstly embark on a thorough analysis seeking to establish the cause, players, issues, positions and ultimate expectations. However, in trying to attain all the desired goals, there were several hurdles both within the structure and outside.

Challenges to Conflict Resolution

The African approach to conflict resolution was not without its own challenges. They varied from structural, political, economic, and social to religious. From the onset, Europeans wanted to weaken Africans' social, political and economic organisation; structurally by war and land grabs, fiscally by taxation, and juridically by contract and pass system amongst others. According to Ingham, it was not smooth having envoys accepted easily in alien territory. These envoys had a challenge of meeting the conditionalities of their presence in an alien territory in terms of beliefs and setting as well as in the comprehension of their loaded tasks[105]. Like it has been indicated above, envoys also had several other responsibilities; declared: representation of the sending state or chief and improving relations and undeclared: espionage.

Linguistic barrier was also a recorded challenge in conflict resolution in the early states in Zimbabwe. At first, there were distinct states and communities based on ethnic and language backgrounds thus making effective communication a serious hindrance. In cases where the dialects were almost similar, there would be some interpretation difficulties. There was also a case where the Ndebele groups wanted to interact with the Shona groups over some noted conflicts. Without adequate interaction and language acquisition, it was impossible to relate well.

[105] Ingham, K (ed.) (1974). The Foreign Relations of African States, London.

There was also a barrier associated with time management and recording. Because early societies had no scientific systems of recording time and events on the ground, it was difficult to relate events to the actual time of occurrence. The few systems of recording their activities were a preserve of the few iterate so to speak, who could put graphically on rocks in caves. Some of these artworks are only being deciphered through carbon dating and other scientific modes of exploration, which unfortunately do not give very accurate information with regards to dates, venues and names amongst others. Some of the methods that were used in most communities to resolve conflicts were not flexible to adapt to time and context. Adaptation involves virility of existing values and practices, tolerance, receptivity, and preparedness to cooperate. However, some of the resolution methods that were applicable in one region could not be effectively applied in another because of language, culture, values and economic activities like farming seasons and trading routines.

While most traditional societies believed in the use of mediation as an effective conflict resolution strategy, it had also over the period presented its problems. It had been noted that the mediation process was involving and cumbersome in early Shona societies as it was not simple for the mediators to please the expectations of the participants to the conflict due to the diversity in cultural, religious and varying other socio-economic factors. The other challenge that also affected the effectiveness of mediation as a process was related to the development of confidence and maintaining the uprightness of the mediators. This emanated from that since mediators were also fellow villagers who had their own social weaknesses, fellow members of the community tended to judge their competence based on their prior knowledge and historical failures. While corruption and bribery were not as pronounced as they are in the modern days, there were also isolated individuals who exposed the renowned mediators to serious temptations in the form of bribery and in some cases, offers of sexual favours.

Some of the challenges that were experienced with mediation also affected the process of arbitration. Acceptability of the resolutions and verdicts made by the arbitrators by all the involved parties to the conflict was analogous to the degree of their honour. Similarly, the trouble in defining the wherewithal of decision making was another argument that the people used to doubt the credibility of the verdicts. It was expected that all the drivers of the conflict resolution processes had enough and credible understanding and information of the practices and norms with regards to the respective process viz-a-viz its culture. This depth of knowledge and experience played very fundamental roles as other conflicts escaped appropriate scrutinisation in accordance with the respective practices and norms.

The effectiveness of most of the early systems of conflict resolution was seriously eroded by several factors amongst them the coming of the Europeans who brought with them globalisation, modernity, alien religions and the new forms of the media. As soon as the Europeans established their settlements, they cheated their sincerity by adopting indigenous identities thereby winning the hearts and minds of the local leadership and the spiritual community. The new settlements gradually drew the indigenous societies closer to the alien practices that appeared to be easy and superb.

First and foremost, it was the Europeans' efficient and luxurious form of transportation which convinced the indigenous people to think that the West was the best. Following this conviction, was the supply of the local military with equally more efficient arms, the supply of the local entertainment with clear liquor and advanced clothing amongst others. Eventually, some indigenous leaders attracted and impressed by the European luxuries accepted to be assimilated into the foreign Christian religion before their identities were also changed. What the Europeans knew was that the local people wanted luxurious and imported goodies and so began to spoil the converted as a way of gradually luring more people to follow suit. The strategy worked as more people like the Mutapa royal family including some spirit mediums like Sekuru Kaguvi got baptised. Generally Shona and Ndebele cultures were decried as worthless by the authorities so much so that they went as far as controlling marriages. Polygynous marriages were penalized by the Tax Ordinance of 1901 while the custom of female child betrothal '*kuzvarira*' was outlawed and the payment of *lobola* was restricted by the Native Marriages Ordinance of 1901. These efforts by the Europeans to some extent watered down the relevance of the local traditions and belief systems.

The globalisation argument also ensured that some form of formal education was introduced as a way of guaranteeing effective communication and assimilation of the locals into the foreign cultures. To ensure that more people mastered the art of communicating in some European languages, some individuals especially those who served as religious catechists, cooks and security aides would be taken to the ports and other far away stations where they would perfect their communication through interaction with the other servants.

Globalization promoted new methods of migration that forced the locals to pursue better economic opportunities in other areas especially across the borders. The deteriorating economic conditions and political insecurity also pushed the best-educated indigenous people to work outside of their homes and neighborhoods in search of more paying jobs so that they could meet some of the new regime's tax requirements. For most of these migrants, it was a response to the struggle against both devastating insufficiency and hidden and overt systems of political subjugation. At the end of it, people's customs and practices were washed to the peri-phery as the new settlements offered completely new and different approaches to lifestyles which unexpectedly stunned the migrants so much so that they had to abandon their original traditional practices.

The coming of the Europeans into Zimbabwe created conflicts social, religious and economic that also led to some communities moving from their original homes to other areas. To some extent, these forms of migration disintegrated the long-held cultural practices and family bonds. It is evident from the weaknesses in some conflict resolution practices that migration; assimilation into other cultures, break-up in families, desecration of family ancestors and the sacrilege of the traditional shrines really rendered these practices irrelevant and ineffective. Some areas had strict regulations regarding some practices and ways of doing business (taboos) so much so that when other people moved into the area, their traditional practices were limited or banned completely. Eventually, such limitations would gradually erode societal customs and belief systems.

Migration also fueled the erosion of indigenous conflict resolution and other valuable systems in that as people were required to pay taxes, they had to seek employment which was not always in their neighbourhood. Sometimes, labourers would be taken to places far away from their homes and these assignments would take long periods of time stretching from six months to a year. One of the noted policies with European employment then was that there was no recognition of the need for family systems each time men were taken away on assignments. Therefore, for the entire period that men were away, it meant that there would be no responsible and appropriate figures to sustain some of the cultural practices that were under men's armpits. It was also realized that wherever the labour force was taken, they would be mixed with others from different cultural, ethnic and social backgrounds thus watering down the values and significance of the cultural belief systems. The conditions of women also worsened because absent spouses who migrated to other areas as labour force for long periods frequently abandoned their social, economic and religious responsibilities. Therefore, economic vicissitudes developing from migration literally pressured women to assume their husbands' roles of providing for their children's sustenance either through food mobilisation or off-field income-creation initiatives. This also to some extent helped erode some of the most important cultural practices.

There was also another strategy that was used by Europeans that the more one got perfect in their culture, the more one got closer to them, and the more one appreciated their practices, the more one got superior and went up the structural ladder of socio-economic rankings. Therefore, more people dreamt of achieving more so that they could be rated better in society. This strategy was employed during the period when modernisation was beginning to claim some space on the local scene. Resultantly, it meant that people expected to benefit in the form of clothing and other assortments.

During the late 1890s, there was also a trend that was forced on the indigenous population through the imposition of some labour and tax laws. The laws that were put in place required the indigenous people to pay taxes to the new governing system of the Europeans. The tax was to be in monetary form. Unfortunately, because the traditional social and economic system relied on barter trade and had never created money, there was nowhere the local people could have gotten the required money. What the Europeans clearly knew was that the requirement would eventually force all and sundry to seek employment from the same Europeans so that they could be paid in monetary form and subsequently be able to pay the taxes. In some cases though, some labourers would just exchange their labour for the required taxes. It was this form of forced labour which marked the genesis of the development of Zimbabwe in general and its people in particular from the Iron Age systems and illiteracy era to a modern and globalized system[ix]. The modern but forced form of labour gradually led to the erosion of some social, religious, political and economic practices including the most revered conflict resolution systems. If anything, the new dispensation actually inculcated a spirit of violence and resistance in the usually quiet and peace-loving people.

Like it has been indicated earlier on that some of the indigenous people envied some of the goods that the Europeans had, it became easy for the latter to manipulate the former using such goods as bait. There were times when some local communities were attacked by other groups destroying their property, livelihoods and losing their sovereignty like what happened when Mzilikazi attacked the Hwata Gwindi at Dandamira hills in 1875 before the latter invited the help of Manuel Antonio de Sousa *Guveya* to provide with guns and ammunition and when Mutapa

Mukombwe sought the help of other neighbouring militaries to fight off an invasion by the Portuguese. These cases show how poverty and lack may sometimes expose people to practices which may be immoral and taboo. Poverty in this case allowed no room for the local people to express their desires and expectations; religious, social, economic and political. It was poverty that allowed the Europeans to squeeze out most of the indigenous cultural practices in exchange for fancy good like clothes, jewellery and glass and defensive materials like guns and ammunition.

National Spirits

I wish to point out that the recognition of some spirits in the administration of land and other resources caused some challenges in resolving conflicts. First and foremost, it is important to understand that there was no single spirit that served the entire land, from the north to the south. Rather, each kingdom had its spirits that guided its interests and communicated with respective ancestral spirits. The communication conducted by spirit mediums is strictly along totemic lines. Therefore, no one spirit could cover the entire land. However, there were some grand spirits that could cover a relatively large area and these would in most cases be close to the kings and therefore protecting the interests of the royal family. Protecting the royal interests could then be taken to mean protecting the national interests which is then completely wrong. Failure to identify areas that were covered by these spirits usually created conflicts either amongst the spirits or between the kingdoms. Some of the spirit mediums that were responsible for particular areas included the following: Nehanda Nyakasikana for the Mutapa area/northern plateau, Chaminuka and Kaguvi in the central plateau, Kinjikitile and Mkwati in the Ndebele area and Nyamandoto in the eastern Manica plateau.

I wish to clarify that Nehanda spirit was not a national figure. Rather, when the ZANLA forces; Mayor Urimbo, Joseph Chimurenga, John Mataure, and Siyangapi Muzhamba (Joseph Khumalo) and others entered into Rhodesia from Zambia through an area called Kakwidze during the formative years of the liberation struggle, they first got in touch with the people in Mt Darwin, Muzarabani and Guruve. These people fell under the traditional Mutapa area which was administered by Nehanda born Mazviona Kawanzaruwa of the Chienderamwano clan in Gonono, Guruve area who apparently lived in Tsokoto area adjacent to Musengezi River near Chimutumbi pool under Chief Matsiwo. This medium was estimated to be over 105 years old and was blind[106]. Coincidentally, upon arrival along the Rhodesia/Zambia border, they

---

[106] Author interviewed some local leaders including Chief Matsiwo and Kraal-head Chidodo and Village-head Tafi on the Mozambican side and attended several traditional ceremonies presided over by the local spirit mediums including Chipfeni, Nyamuseve, Chidyamauyu and Chiodzamamera in 1994, 1995 and 2000 meant to identify the real spirit medium of Nehanda before crossing the border to Chief Makombe in Tete, Mozambique. Author visited Chimutumbi pool along Musengezi River and Mbuya Nehanda's Hut in Tsokoto in 1994 and also attended a 30-day appeasement of the dead ceremony at Shavarunzi by the Mbari clan led by Majuru, a direct descendant of the Nehanda family where over 3000 graves were identified. Author has firsthand experience with the Nehanda spirit.

were referred to Mbuya Nehanda by spirit media Sekuru Chipfeni, Sekuru Chidyamauyu and Sekuru Chiodzamamera[x]. Chipfeni was a distant relative of Nehanda spirit medium. Their recognition and adherence to the practices dictated by Nehanda presented a somewhat national position as ZANLA's cause eventually became national. These early combatants were impressed by Nehanda that they eventually included her role in the national education curriculum depicting her as a national spirit and yet, she had only helped in the northern activities around Guruve, Muzarabani and Mt Darwin where ZANLA had operated. ZIPRA had operated in the north-west and western parts of Rhodesia where other spirit mediums had also helped.

Summary

Conflict resolution is a practice that is part and parcel of any progressive society. No community would allow conflicts to devastate what would have been built. However, despite having several of these conflict resolution methods, there are also challenges that equally affect their effective application. The chapter has explained several of the challenges recorded in the history of conflicts in Zimbabwe. The identified challenges range from governance, cultural, traditional, and personal up to structural. The involvement of traditional spirits and their mediums have also been discussed as they are critical in the lives of the indigenous Africans.

---

[i] Guruuswa is an imaginary country which is said to be the original land for the Bantu people. Some people believe it is in North Africa while others think it is in Tanzania.

[ii] I also support the argument that the people who lived in the early states in Zimbabwe were backward. I still present the same argument that there are some people who are still backward mainly because of the prevailing economic and political circumstances. People are still fetching water from the bush, fetching firewood from the jungle and being subjected to ancient conditions and practices that qualify for the lowest stages of development.

[iii] Before the coming of the Europeans, there was a place called Mazowi, named after a river that flows from Chinamhora/Seke confluence right down to Zambezi River. The Europeans corrupted the name to Mazoe before it was later changed to Mazowe after the 1980 political

independence. Mazowe District now houses Christon Bank (Shavarunzi), Mvurwi, Dandamera (Dandamira), and Chiweshe areas.

[iv] It is Dark era because these societies had not yet seen and embraced civilization and development which ultimately brought them to the present world of technology and at the pace that they have evolved and developed. This may invite nasty contradictions with some scholars and politicians choosing to differ and justifying the 'backwardness' that characterised the indigenous people. I remain steadfast that indeed Africa and its people were behind technologically.

[v] Nehanda is believed to have been a daughter of the founding ancestor of the Mutapa dynasty during the 15th century. It is believed that she sexually indulged with her brother as a way of securing spiritual power for the founding of a powerful kingdom by her father. It was after her death that she became a *mhondoro*.

[vi] Some spirits and cultural analysts argue that the fact that another voice reincarnated on Mativira in 1906 barely nine years after the execution of Charwe is an indication that the Nehanda spirit was angry about what the medium had done. Traditionally, it is believed that ancestral spirits are sacred and pure and therefore do not condone evil and dirty activities. In 1896, Charwe was charged for allegedly ordering the killing of H. M. Pollard Kanyaira by Hwata at Shop for losing her carrier which Charwe had given to the latter. The 1897 court ruling led to the execution of Charwe at Causeway Fort. In the eyes of the ordinary people, it was taken as if she was charged for allegedly inciting the resistance to taxation and European invasion. It was therefore this argument by some spirits that Charwe had indeed murdered Pollard hence the anger by

Nehanda and the subsequent reincarnation in Mativirira. Some present day politicians especially during the second Chimurenga believed that Charwe had been executed for inciting fellow country people to resist European invasion. This view and position by the politicians was only an abuse of the people's ignorance and the desire to politicize an unfortunate past for the benefit of the liberation struggle during the 1960s to the 1970s.

[vii] In 1561, Father Goncalo da Silveira baptised Mapunzagutu as *Dom Sebastiao* (Lord Sebastian) and his mother as *Dona Maria* (Lady Mary) after the Virgin Mary. Following this, between 250 and 300 other people including men of rank in the state were baptized to Roman Catholicism.

[viii] The reduction in Africans in employment and the low numbers of primary school graduates proceeding into secondary is according to other scholars attributed to the intensification of the liberation war in the 1970s. It is argued that while some students voluntarily joined the war, the majority were either forced or joined as an escape from criminal and failed past. Bhebhe (1999) talks about how Rex Nhongo of ZANLA and Dube of ZIPRA kidnapped school children for the liberation struggle. The Secretary for African Education in Smith regime reported that in 1977, there were 398 primary schools with 74 000 pupils and 14 secondary schools with 3685 pupils which closed as a result of the liberation war. This, in the absence of a scientific study does not however mean the students had crossed the borders for the liberation struggle; it may point to the persecution levels by the two warring parties on the innocent and defenceless citizens.

[ix] Though this was forced labour, it helped the development and growth

of the Zimbabwean infrastructure and its people. The Europeans had realized that the local people were stuck to some cultural beliefs which did not allow them to abandon their bad and backward past for anything new and productive. Indigenous people had to be forced to work for their development, so believed the Europeans.

[x] The other ZANLA members who attended a meeting with Mbuya Nehanda in 1972 at Chifombo after Nehanda had been secretly smuggled out of Rhodesia by Mayor Urimbo, Joseph Chimurenga, John Mataure, and Siyangapi Muzhamba were Kenny Ridzai, Chinodakufa, Hebert Chitepo, Noel Mukono, Josiah Tongogara, Chimurenga, Dabulamanzi, Chinamaropa, Rusununguko Kadungure, and Chauke amongst others.

9 781729 044810